Castlederg
and
Victoria
Bridge
Tramway

Dr E M Patterson, DSc, MRIA, FRSE

Colourpoint Books

It was with considerable sadness that Colourpoint Books learned of the death of Dr E M Patterson, early in 1997, during the preparation of this book. The contribution of Dr Patterson to research on Irish railway history has been enormous, and it is fitting that the publication of his last book should proceed as planned, in accordance with the wishes of his daughter, Mrs Anna Singer. The manuscript is essentially as Dr Patterson left it, with some additional material on the Act of Parliament authorising the line, by Michael Pollard of Omagh, who had assisted Dr Patterson with his research. We are also indebted to Michael for giving us access to his photographic collection for this book.

Dr E M Patterson, at Tiriach, Pitlochry, Perthshire, Scotland in October 1995

© Dr E M Patterson
    Newtownards
    1998

Designed by Colourpoint Books, Newtownards

Printed by ColourBooks

ISBN 1 898392 29 3

Colourpoint Books
Unit D5, Ards Business Centre
Jubilee Road
NEWTOWNARDS
Co Down
N Ireland
BT23 4YH
Tel: (01247) 820505 / 819787 Ex 239
Fax: (01247) 821900
E-mail: Info@colourpoint.co.uk
Web-site: www.colourpoint.co.uk

Front cover inset photograph:
Builder's record of 0-4-4T No 5 'Castlederg' in works grey livery.

Rear cover:
Top: *Former GNR Station-master's house, Victoria Bridge.*

Centre: *Restored CVBT carriage No 4, UFTM*

Bottom: *Castlederg station today*
Michael Pollard

Contents

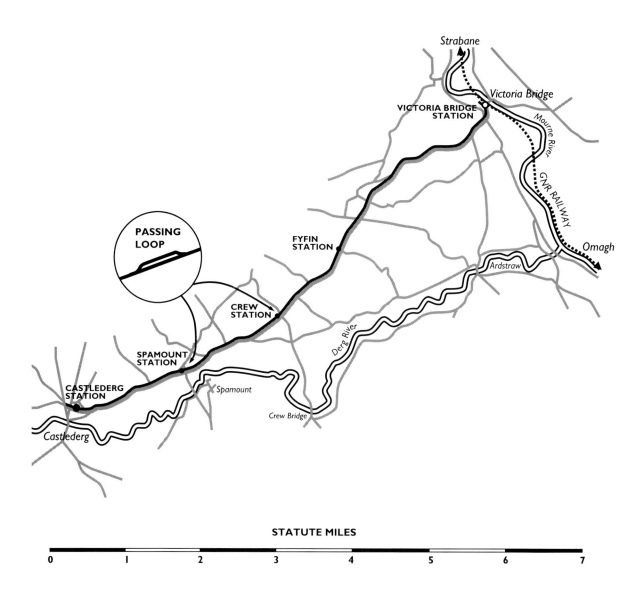

STATUTE MILES

0   1   2   3   4   5   6   7

The route of the Castlederg and Victoria Bridge Tramway

Introduction

T HE CASTLEDERG AND Victoria Bridge Tramway was one of the smallest of the independent Irish narrow-gauge railway systems, only the Portstewart, Bessbrook and Lucan being smaller. It lay to the west of the Great Northern Railway Company's standard gauge line from Portadown to Londonderry and its existence spanned the short period of 49 years.

The tramway connected the village of Castlederg with the outside world by way of the Great Northern's wayside station at Victoria Bridge but, since there were few commuters and only one manufacturing concern in Castlederg itself, the connection was scarcely a busy one. Periodic cattle fairs and markets in Castlederg generated bursts of business, whilst at other times the traffic was light and easily organised.

To understand the raison d'etre of the tramway and how it functioned, we have first to consider its geographical and historic setting, cradled as it was among quiet hills, close to the Tyrone-Donegal border, a county boundary that became an international one in 1921 on the creation of the Irish Free State. The county of Tyrone, within which the tramway operated, has an area of 779,563 acres (1218 square miles), making it the largest of the six

counties that at present form Northern Ireland. Within the county, Castlederg was peripheral and its hinterland was not heavily populated. The 7¼ miles of the tramway traversed agricultural country without any intermediate villages and was scarcely promising ground in which to generate heavy railway traffic.

Above: Victoria Bridge station on 5 August 1958, looking north.
The CVBT platform was to the left of the station building.

$\widehat{1}$

Regional Setting

DERG IS A word of native Irish origin, meaning red or ruddy. In the Scottish Gaelic it would be spelt 'dearg', and its appellation to the lough, river and castle in north-west Ireland may well refer to the colour of the autumnal and winter vegetation on the mountains that surround the lough and flank the river valley.

The River Derg originates from the north-east corner of Lough Derg, a stretch of water two miles across, set high among the mountains of Donegal. The Lough is shallow and contains no less than 46 islands, many of them tiny and insignificant, but two of them possess special archeological and historical interest. These are named Station Island and Saint's Island. An early monastic settlement is believed to have been sited on Saint's Island, which was formerly named St Dabheoc's Island. The purpose of this Prior was to minister to the needs of pilgrims travelling to the cave known as St Patrick's Purgatory on Station Island, a mile to the east. In the middle ages pilgrimages to Lough Derg became famous throughout Europe. An ancient roadway from the village of Pettigo to the shore of the lough passes Rathnacross, an old hill fort, and an ancient church and burial ground at Templecairn.[1] Today the surface of Saint's Island is uneven and greatly overgrown, with earthen banks, dry stone structures and grave slabs. By contrast pilgrimage traffic is now centred on Station Island, where much of the available area is taken up by the Basilica and administrative buildings that were erected there in the early part of this century.

The rocks around Lough Derg are like those of the western Scottish Highlands. Moinian Rocks, known as granulites, lie under and around the Lough and are succeeded by Dalradian mica-schists where the River Derg makes its way to the north-east. Several miles down stream much younger sandstones of Carboniferous age appear and a hard bed among

Station Island (left) and Saint's Island,, Lough Derg.   (Numbers in bold type refer to books listed on page 95.)

them was quarried at a time to provide millstones.[2]

The River Derg is only half a mile old where it crosses the county boundary between Donegal and Tyrone. Four miles on, the Glendergan River tumbles in on the left bank, descending from Little Lough Bradan. Seven miles on, as the crow flies, the Mourne Beg River forms another left-bank confluent. The intervening miles of the Derg are exceedingly meandering because of the lessening gradient of the river bed. The valley broadens, mountains are left behind and, a couple of miles from Mourne Beg Bridge, the river flows past the town of Castlederg, its major part being on the left or northern bank. Seven miles on, the Derg passes the tiny cross-roads village of Ardstraw and, after a further one and a half miles, it joins the River Strule, their union forming the River Mourne. Two and a half miles downstream from this junction is Victoria Bridge, where the Castlederg Tram found itself beside the Great Northern Railway. With a catchment covering half of County Tyrone, the Strule-Mourne River was fast flowing and, after heavy rains, was liable to flood across the flat land on each side. Five miles north of Victoria Bridge stands the town of Strabane. Here the Mourne River is joined by the considerable River Finn. the combination being named the River Foyle, practically at sea-level. The city and port of Londonderry, Derry for short, is fourteen miles to the north.

Returning to the River Derg, we find that its elevation when leaving Lough Derg is close to 500 feet above sea level. Along its 13 mile course to Castlederg it drops to an elevation of 150 feet, a fall of around 27 feet per mile. Continuing to the north-east its gradient slackens, and over 7 miles its elevation has fallen to 100 feet, a fall of only 7 feet per mile. Its confluence with the River Strule lies a mile and a half from the tiny village of Ardstraw. Two miles to the north lies Victoria Bridge, an inconsequential place that took its name from a road bridge crossing the Mourne, constructed in Queen Victoria's reign.

Having placed Castlederg in County Tyrone, let us consider how the village began. It would appear that Castlederg originated during the Plantation of Ulster [3] out of the grant of 2000 acres of land in 1609 by the English King James I (James VI of Scotland) to one Sir John Davis or Davies, an English lawyer who had become attorney-general for Ireland. Shortly after this grant, and certainly before 1619, Sir John Davis built, as he was statutorily required to do, a simple castle or tower-house of 'lyme and stone', the purpose of which was to defend the settlement, which held sixteen British immigrant families. To facilitate movement, and to protect his lands, Davis erected a simple bridge of stone over the River Derg. It was the first time that the Derg had been bridged and the hamlet that grew up beside the castle came first to be called Derg Bridge, and later Castlederg.

Davis received a further grant of land at a place called Claraghmore, some 8 miles to the south-east of Castlederg. There he built a second castle, variously named Kerlis, Kirlish or Curlews. Davis was actively aware of the strategic value of a good road and he linked his castles of Derg and Kerlis by a stone causeway, 8 feet in width and 7 miles in length, its course passing in a straight line, like a Roman road, over Mulnavat Hill and across peaty bog land. Fragments of this causeway are still traceable, while some of it has been remade into the present county road, linking Castlederg and the little village of Drumquin.

The history of Castlederg has been turbulent. Before the settlement had been long in existence, the native Irish expressed their resentment of the English colonisation of Tyrone and, in a rebellion in 1641, Sir Phelim O'Neill laid siege to the castle of Derg. Though

O'Neill failed to take the castle and he and his forces were eventually driven off with considerable loss of men, horses and ammunition. The castle and the houses of the little settlement were alike so greatly injured that the castle was never rebuilt. To this day it stands as a compact, picturesque ruin on the north bank of the river, a short way upstream from the road bridge. That bridge is in fact the second one on the site. Davis's original bridge did duty until 1835, by which date it was showing signs of failing under increasingly heavy traffic, and it was totally rebuilt.

Castlederg in the 1950s, looking towards William Street. In the distance the CVBT station is visible. The tramway entered the square through the gateway visible directly above the lady crossing the road, and terminated to the right of the picture.

HN STREET, CASTLEDERG, CO.TYRONE

In spite of the evolution in the 18th and early 19th centuries of a local network of roads [4], only two of them attained any local importance. The first of these ran south west to the tiny village of Ederny, the second went north east to the similarly sized Ardstraw. Davis's old 'causeway' to his Kirlish Castle was replaced by a less hilly minor road to the villages of Drumquin and Dromore, but its north-westerly prolongation was inhibited by the presence of part of the Sperrin Mountains, lying south of the River Finn. The upgrading of a host of tertiary roads was inhibited by the creation of the inter-state border which insisted on the use of 'approved roads', where a customs post was sited, and along which cross-border traffic became canalised to facilitate customs examination.

Compared to many other towns in Ulster, the growth rate of Castlederg during the tramway years was insignificant. At the 1831 census it held 875 persons, and fifty years later, just before the tramway was created, the total had fallen to 756. The turn of the century (1901 census) recorded 761 persons, a fall from the 796 at the 1891 census. Upward growth was resumed in the first decade of the 20th century, bringing the population of the little town to 835 in 1911. It became 891 in the 1961 census but by then the tram was dead and gone. It had effectively done nothing towards the establishment of new industries or creating new traffic along the road to Victoria Bridge.

The Mourne-Strule valley saw the Londonderry and Enniskillen Railway establish an iron road between Londonderry, Strabane and Omagh in 1852, opening a station at Victoria Bridge, a site chosen because an isolated road bridge crossed the Mourne River there, leading east into the foothills of the main mass of the Sperrin Mountains. The next river crossing was five miles upstream at the market town of Newtownstewart.

Many years before the initiation of the Castlederg and Victoria Bridge Tramway scheme, the United Kingdom government attempted to assist the depressed economy of Ireland by promoting the development of rail transport. The depression began in the famine years of 1845-1849, when the potato harvest repeatedly failed. The inexpensive potato was the basic food crop of the bulk of the population. Starvation and attendant disease caused the death of over a million people in Ireland. Minor potato crop failures had occurred before, but the immensity of the tragedy of the 1840s was unprecedented. Reluctantly the British Parliament realised that Ireland's problem, apart from chronic over-population, stemmed from the fact that the country's unbalanced economy depended on agriculture. In mainland Britain, railway mileage was growing rapidly, and industries were apparently activated by having access to rail services. Therefore simplistically, the provision of railways in the remoter parts of Ireland would necessarily bring industry and commerce where neither had existed before. A general Act of Parliament was therefore enacted in 1860 which simplified the construction of roadside tramways, avoiding the sundry expenses attendant on a local and personal Act. The Act had little practical effect because only animal power was permitted for traction. An Amending Act in the following year merely made trivial alterations in the procedure for applications.

In the attitude of Parliament, caution was the operative word, and not until 1871 were roadside tramways allowed to employ mechanical power. Even then the relaxation was hedged about with restrictions. Though main line trains were running at a mile a minute in places, the roadside tramways had a statutory maximum speed of 6 miles an hour in open roads in rural areas, and of only 3 mph in urban areas. The only available mechanical power was the ubiquitous steam engine, as motorised or electrical power was unknown. The concept of steam-hauled tramcars proceeding at a funeral pace, being passed by fast walkers and left far behind by people pedalling bicycles, was hardly calculated to appeal to promoters and critical investors, even if horses were not unduly alarmed. Yet, a bait was eventually offered to backers by the provision of a 'baronial guarantee' of fixed interest on all or part of the invested capital (a 'barony' was a subdivision of a county, larger than a parish; a 'guarantee' was a charge on ratepayers living in the barony). Progress was terribly slow, and a further twelve years ground by before further stimulus was offered to investors through the 1883 Tramways and Public Companies (Ireland) Act (46-47 Vict, chapt XLIII) which offered state assistance as a guarantee to the baronies. Though it was nearly 40 years since the potato famine, governments were careful that their generosity was not abused. The complicated preliminary procedures still existed, and put the promoters to initial heavy expense even before the purchase of land was met, and absorbed capital that would have been better spent on basics, such as less severe gradients and heavier permanent way.

2

Things Begin To Move

OVER THE YEARS writers have referred to Sir Robert Ferguson, then M P for Derry City, saying that in 1860 he had sponsored a Bill in the British Parliament which resulted in the 1860 Tramway Act being passed. This fact appears to have been unjustifiably extended and in 1884, when the Castlederg Tramway was being opened, the Marquis of Hamilton commented in his speech that Sir Robert had "been largely instrumental in securing the Act" in 1860 for the construction of a railway between Castlederg and Victoria Bridge station but, since that gentleman died on 13 March 1860, the matter had been left in abeyance. Ferguson was likewise reputed to have had a survey of the line of railway made at his own expense. Under Ferguson's plan, and in conformity with the conditions of the 1860 Tramways Act, it was the intention to build the line within 30 feet of the middle of the public roadway. However, there is no mention of this scheme in contemporary newspapers, nor is there any trace of it in the House of Lords Record Office files.

From 9 May 1852 rail services were available through Victoria Bridge on the Londonderry & Enniskillen Railway. From 1876-1883 this company's line was rented by the Great Northern Railway, and was then amalgamated with it. The station yard at Victoria Bridge was used to stable the horses and the vehicles that streamed in from Castlederg and beyond.

Inevitably, the people of Castlederg clamoured for a railway to connect with the Great Northern line, that was only 7¼ miles distant. The village merchants depended on local carriers to get goods to and from Castlederg and they were convinced that a branch railway from Victoria Bridge would break the carriers' monopoly, and could only be of benefit to the trade of the area. Initially, they had grandiose notions and visualised a standard gauge branch line that would run through Castlederg and on to Donegal town. There would certainly have been opposition to such a line from the Finn Valley Railway, at that time a standard gauge line from Stranorlar to Strabane.

Hence when the scheme was costed, the sights of the promoters were lowered, and a line terminating at Castlederg was targeted. There would have been difficulty in securing a County Guarantee, so sights were again lowered and the promoters then considered the feasibility of a roadside steam tramway, built to the narrow gauge of 3 feet, aided by the powers of the 1871 Tramways Act. The next stage was the convening of a preliminary public meeting in the Ferguson Arms Hotel, Castlederg on 21 August 1881. Those present were Dr Leary, Messrs J R Johnson, Andrew Gailey (Senior & Junior), W G McHugh, John Burke, James McGaw, A Adams and T P Woods. The professional services of Mr J G Barton, civil engineer, had been secured and he attended. An executive committee was formed, with power to summon further meetings and to liaise with the GNR (I). The committee consisted of three Justices of the Peace (Captain Montgomery Stewart, William King and Charles Love), the manager of the local branch of the Ulster Bank, Mr S P Woods, Messrs, A Andrews, Messrs Burke and Curran, Andrew Gailey (Sen), Andrew Gailey (Jun), Wm Gamble, Wm & James McCormack, James McCoy, Robert McCoy, Wm McErvel, Thomas Kerrigan and N Roleston.

Just how many of these gentlemen were experts in railway organisation is not recorded but they represented a good cross-section of the hard-headed business community. To steer them through the convolutions of railway business they leaned heavily on the shoulders of their consulting Civil Engineer, J G Barton. At the meeting three resolutions were moved and adopted: (a) The cash lying in the Ulster Bank at Castlederg and totalling about £53.50, transferred to the tramway promoters by the defunct Castlederg and Victoria Bridge Railway, be utilised to cover preliminary expenses of the proposed tramway; (b) a subscription list be opened (c) Mr Barton be instructed to make out the preliminary notices, to publish the same, to make what plans and estimates needed to fulfil the conditions of the Tramway Act of 1860.

To the members of the committee, Mr Barton explained the meaning of the requirements of the 1860 Act and agreed to implement these for the expenses incurred. He said that he would make no personal charge in the event of the scheme falling through. However, if a Provisional Order was eventually obtained, he was to be paid for his time.

At a further meeting, held on 4 November 1881, it was considered that a Rate of 4d in the pound would be required towards the tramway's upkeep. It was decided that a deputation should approach the merchants of Londonderry to seek shareholders amongst them. Illustrative of the hard-headed nature of the Castlederg promoters and their attention to fine detail, they resolved to apply to the General Manager of the Great Northern Railway for a number of free passes to cover the 20 mile trip!

Four days later, at another Committee meeting, it was decided that the Rate to be sought under the Baronial Guarantee should be 6d in the pound. The share list was declared open, and Gilbert McHugh and William King were nominated as directors. A further meeting was held on 20 November, when F Purcell Woods officiated as the Honourary Secretary, and was instructed to obtain a Provisional Order in Council from the Lord Lieutenant. The new secretary reported that the deputation to the Londonderry merchants and to the GNR (Ireland) Railway had yielded encouraging results. Woods gave the directors a typically rosy picture of the tramway's prospects and gave as his opinion, that it was quite certain to make a profit of between £2000 and £3000 a year, adding cautiously that if it only paid £650 a year, which was the interest on the guaranteed shares, the baronial guarantees would never have to be called upon. In spite of these brave words and political self-congratulation, in fact, it was proving difficult to attract capital. The people of Castlederg were obviously happy if a tramway materialised and to make use of it once it was built provided that they did not have to risk any of their own money in the venture.

The fate of the scheme swung in the balance and ten months slipped by before another committee meeting was convened. In the interim, the members resolved to make encouraging sounds and to advance 10 percent of the money on the shares subscribed for by then and thereby to raise the finances for a public bill. The people of Castlederg were again urged to back their local scheme but a proposal to approach the merchants of Derry again was abandoned.

A fortnight passed and at a further meeting of the committee, the names of Major Smyly and of John Henderson, JP were added to the Board. It was decided that the title to be given to the line would be the Castlederg and Victoria Bridge Tramway. Up to them it had been Victoria Bridge and Castlederg Tramway. Active steps were now taken to secure Parliamentary sanction of a Bill for the line. Barton had formalised the tramway into three sections:

Tramway No 1:   From Castlederg station to the goods yard on the west side of Victoria Bridge station: length 7 miles, 5 chains.

Tramway No 2:   An extension from Castlederg station to the adjacent Market Place, formerly known as the Corn Market: length 5 chains (this was later extended).

Tramway No 3:   A short spur from the NE end of Tramway No 1 where it turned into the goods yard at the rear of the down platform of Victoria Bridge station: length 8 chains, 8 yards.

On 13 December 1882 it was decided to construct an additional tramway (No 4), as a branch from Spamount Halt to the spinning mills, then belonging to Messrs Conner. These stood on the southern bank of the River Derg. According to the Parliamentary plans, the branch was to turn abruptly off the main line on a 1 chain curve facing Castlederg. Once across the river the line turned left on a 1½ chain curve and, on the way to the mill building, crossed the mill race on two curves each of 2 chains radius. The length of the Spamount branch was to have been 4 furlongs 40 yards and animal power alone was to be employed. A T Newham has stated that the gradients on the branch were to range from 1 to 23 to 1 in 600. The mill owners were to make themselves responsible for haulage of the wagons on the branch. It is interesting that the parliamentary plan marks a gas works alongside the mill race. It is probable that coal for the manufacture of gas would have accounted for a proportion of the inward traffic on the branch, though by the time it had reached the gas works it would have suffered four handlings and increased considerably in price as a result. The tramway company attempted to make conditions over the branch, the mill not only doing its own haulage but also purchasing £1000 worth of ordinary shares. The latter condition was modified to £1000 of preference and £200 of ordinary shares but, in the event, the branch was never built and the mill owners moved their goods along the existing road by horse and cart, from where a wagon or wagons had been left in the loop on the main line. The tramway company was, in fact, not permitted to issue preference shares and financial arrangements with the Spamount Mills seem to have fallen through.

Unexpectedly, the Great Northern Railway directors then bared their teeth and petitioned Parliament against the building of the tramway. What political moves caused such an action cannot now be discovered but it nearly ended the tramway project. In the event their opposition was short lived and, at the Board Meeting on 9 September, it was

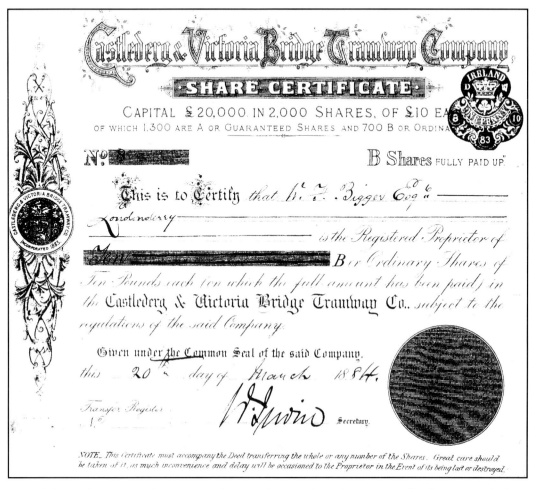

Castlederg & Victoria Bridge Tramway Company

SHARE CERTIFICATE

CAPITAL £20,000. IN 2,000 SHARES, OF £10 EA
OF WHICH 1,300 ARE A OR GUARANTEED SHARES AND 700 B OR ORDINA

Nº 8   **B Shares** FULLY PAID UP.

This is to Certify that *W. F. Bigger Esq*

Londonderry

is the Registered Proprietor of

B or Ordinary Shares of

Ten Pounds each (on which the full amount has been paid) in

the Castlederg & Victoria Bridge Tramway Co. *subject to the*

regulations of the said Company.

Given under the Common Seal of the said Company.

this   *20*   *day of*   *March*   *1884.*

Transfer Register

  W. Irwin   Secretary.

NOTE.— *This Certificate must accompany the Deed transferring the whole or any number of the Shares. Great care should be taken of it, as much inconvenience and delay will be occasioned to the Proprietor in the Event of its being lost or destroyed.*

A Castlederg and Victoria Bridge Tramway share certificate.. It bears the signature of William Irwin, the first secretary.

reported that the Great Northern had withdrawn their opposition. Later indeed they subscribed for £2000 of ordinary shares in the tramway company, the people of Castlederg being persuaded to do the same.

A meeting of the tramway directors took place on 14 June 1883, at which they gave approval to the Company's Bill, as amended by the House of Commons. At the same meeting, Mr Barton was awarded £50 per month for his parliamentary work and, in addition, £130 for his work as a professional engineer. Matters now moved swiftly to a conclusion and on 17 July Barton showed the directors a telegram he had just received from the parliamentary agents, Messrs Martin & Lester, stating that the Company's Bill had received the Royal Assent the previous day.

There are many interesting points in the Act of Parliament:

1   The work must be approved by:
    (a) The Grand Jury of County Tyrone and the County Surveyor.
    (b) Parliament

2   Six Directors were named, Major Smylie, William King, John Herdman, Albert McHugh, William McErvel and Doctor Thomas Leary. A Director must hold at least twenty £10.00 shares.

3   The Company had the right of compulsory purchase of land for a period of two years from the passing of the Act, no more.

4   The tramway was to be completed in four years. If not the guarantee was forfeit.

5   The Barony, ie the Grand Jury, was to guarantee 5% return on £13,000 stock. The remainder of the capital was made up of £7,000 of ordinary shares at 5%. The Baronial guarantee was to last 35 years, ie until 1918.

6   The tramway was to be 3'0" gauge and constructed at the side of the roadway.

7   Every sanitary authority had to have free access to their drains without consent from the Company.

8   Where no footpath existed alongside the road, the tramway was to be left with a surface available for foot passengers to the satisfaction of the County Surveyor. This was to lead to several deaths where people walked along the tramway, got tired and sat down and slept not hearing the tram. From Craigmonaghan to Castlederg the footpath was to be laid by the Company on the opposite side of the road to the tramway.

9   The Company had to construct and maintain level accesses and should a landowner ask for one and obtain approval from the County Surveyor for one it was to be provided, free of charge, and maintained by the Company.

10 All Road crossings were to be level and have wood placed between the rails.

11 Where the tramway was 6 inches or more above the road a kerb was to be laid and the minimum width of road was to be 18 feet. This involved the removal of some fences.

12 Money could not be paid to a shareholder who was a 'minor, idiot or lunatic'; it could be paid to his or her guardian.

13 One often wondered at the elaborate half year statements produced by these railway companies, which followed a very similar format. This Tramway Act sets out a very

elaborate system to assess the affairs of the Company on a six monthly basis involving the Board of Trade and the Grand Jury of Tyrone and the Company. In case of a dispute an arbitrator or an umpire was appointed by the assises. Presumably, all of this was to ensure that the Baronial guarantee was assessed correctly.

14 The Act allowed the tramway to be powered by animal power, steam, electricity or any other mechanical or motive power. Internal combustion engines had not entered the scene but they were in the experimental stage.

15 The Company could charge in accordance with the Tramway Act and each passenger was allowed a personal luggage not exceeding 28 lbs weight, free of charge.

16 The Company could not build at Victoria Bridge without consent in writing from the GNR. This was the one area where compulsory purchase did not apply. Railways, such as the GNR, were very powerful and very much a law onto themselves and obviously the GNR intended to control this tramway.

17 Any dispute between the Company and any landowner or the County Surveyor could be arbitrated by the Board of Works.

18 Should the line be worked by electricity, no interference was to be made to the telegraph line belonging to the Post-Master General. Again the Board of Trade was to arbitrate.

19 The Company, if required, was to carry mails, including parcels for the Post-Master General.

One wonders whether all these regulations relating to a tramway would out-weigh the saving in cost between a tramway and a dedicated railway line.

The Act was passed in July 1883. It was a pity it was not delayed for a few months as the Tramway Act of 1883 would have allowed an annual grant of £260 from the Government.

Backed by their Act of Parliament, the Board elected William King as their Chairman and Gilbert McHugh Vice-Chairman. William Irwin was appointed Secretary and Manager at a salary of £160 per annum. Barton was asked to advertise for tenders to build the station house and goods depot at Castlederg, in William Street. The station contract was given to Hepburn of Strabane. The construction of the line was entrusted to Messrs T I Dixon of Belfast.

3

The Course of the Line

T HE HEADQUARTERS OF the Company were based in Castlederg in a substantial building of red brick. Living accommodation for the only stationmaster on the line was in a single bay, two storey section which had abutting ranges of single storey construction that housed offices, stores and waiting rooms. A short way to the east of the station buildings was a two road gable-ended building that was both an engine shed and the repair shop. At its west end a water tank was raised on a stone-built pillar. The platform was at ground level, on the south side of the line. Close to the west end of the station building, a bell hung from a bracket on a post and is believed to have been rung to warn passengers of the imminent departure of a train.

Castlederg station in 1933, looking east towards Victoria Bridge. The tramway swung right at the shed to join William Street, visible in the distance. In the foreground is the line which continued to Market Place. The station building still exists today (see rear cover).

LGRP 7115

The 25 inch Ordnance Survey plan (Tyrone 16-9) shows a turntable just west of the engine shed but its use must have been confined to the early years, when only engine Nos 1-3 were in use. Its diameter was about nine feet, just sufficient to hold the Kitson engines. Since there is no record of a matching turntable at Victoria Bridge, there could not have been a regular practice of working funnel-first in both directions. In the event, the rolling stock had their wheels shielded on one side only, towards the road.

The engine shed at Castlederg, on the same occasion as the photograph opposite. Each road could accommodate two engines.

Real Photographs 4972

From the station yard, an end-on siding "Tramway No 2" went to Castlederg market, passing the police barrack and along John Street for a total distance of 8 chains 78 yards, according to the plan attached to the Parliamentary Bill, but 8 chains 87 yards on the Great Northern gradient plan. The latter diagram shows a fall of 1 in 110 along the market branch. The said Act defined the market branch as "Tramway No 2 single line five chains in length wholly situate in the townland of Churchtown and parish of Urney commencing by a junction with Tramway No 1 at its termination above described and terminating in the Castle Market-square." The length of the market branch seems to be in some doubt, as it may have been extended after the line was built.

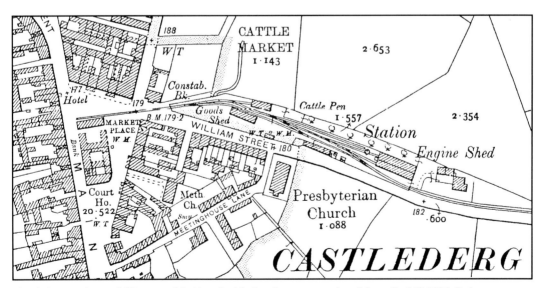

Castlederg station and 'Tramway No 2' to the Market Square. reproduced from the 25" 1906 Ordnance Survey map, Tyrone. Reproduced 80% scale.

A rare view of a train at the market Square in Castlederg, looking north towards the Commercial Hotel side of the square. The engine is the Beyer Peacock 2-4-0T, with wagon No 1 attached. One of the four top flaps is open and cattle visible inside.
Courtesy Scott McFarland

Castlederg on 6 August 1930, looking east. 2-6-0T No 5 is on the left and No 4 is arriving in from Victoria Bridge with a train. It is passing through the metal gates that gave access from William Street.
H C Casserley 7022

The station buildings at Castlederg separated the railway yard from the public road, named William Street and security was provided by metal gates at each end of the yard. The level of the yard was 182′ above Ordnance Datum. Where the line emerged from the east end of the yard, the rails were on the north side of the road. A quarter mile out, Strabane Road trailed in on the right, forming a road fork at 177′ OD. The line then began to climb steeply, passing the Rectory on a stretch of 1 in 36, and then rising to a minor summit beside Riverside Manse at 288′ OD with two short stretches at 1 in 36 and 1 in 38. Over the 1¾ mile section to the first halt, named Spamount, there were 22 changes of gradient, reflecting the fact that the line was laid directly on the existing road, with the minimum of engineering work.

It was at Spamount halt that Tramway No 4 was to have gone to the woollen mills across the River Derg. As mentioned above, the branch tramway to the mill was not built but a loop was substituted. A wooden hut was provided for shelter and clerical assistance was furnished, for many years, by a Miss Cecily Gollagher. She had originally come from

A tram on the outskirts of Castlederg, heading towards Victoria Bridge. Nearest the camera is a panelled carriage, probably the now preserved No 4, preceded by bogie third No 5 and a brake van.
Michael Pollard collection

In the first of two views at Spamount, we see a Victoria Bridge-bound train, possibly the 08.15, hauled by No 5. Note the passing loop. The train consists of wagon No 12, a brake van, a four-wheeled carriage and the bogie carriage.
Kenn Nunn collection, courtesy LCGB

In the opposite direction comes a Castlederg-bound train, also with No 5. this train is made up of six wagons, a coach and a brake van.
Mrs E Wilson (Michael Pollard collection)

Tory Island, eleven miles off the coast of north-west Donegal. She lived in a nearby cottage and was a fluent Irish speaker. Miss Gollagher opened and closed the hut, took advice notes and waybills mostly connected with the mill traffic, made her self generally useful and, as a profitable sideline, knitted woollen cardigans.

Leaving Spamount halt, the tramway began a fairly steady ascent for a mile and a quarter. None of the climb was particularly steep, apart from 250 yards at 1 in 60, which brought the line up to an altitude of 200' OD, a quarter of a mile to the east of Spamount.

Crew halt (styled 'Crew Station' on the 6" Ordnance map) lay 3¾ miles from Castlederg on a rise of 1 in 44. As at Spamount, there was a loop and a railway shelter that was looked after by a retired farmer named Allen. The halt was never referred to as Crew by local people, but always as 'Charlie Allen's'. The inevitable jokes perpetrated by journalists about the confusion between Crew and Crewe, when passengers asked for tickets, were probably apocryphal.

Crew halt in the early days of the tramway, showing No 3, one of the 0-4-0T locomotives heading towards Castlederg. Some wit has added the sign board to the negative, no doubt for comparison with 'Crewe' in England, a station at the opposite end of the size spectrum from 'Crew' in Co Tyrone.

Michael Pollard collection

About a hundred yards beyond Crew came the steepest part of the tramway which rose at 1 in 31 for around 150 yards and was compounded by a 6 chain curve. A climb continued, made up of 1 in 46/43/37/102 which lifted the tramway to its summit 4½ miles out of Castlederg, at an elevation of just on 300' OD. The tramway had gained 118 feet in height since leaving Castlederg.

From the summit, there was an unbroken descent to Victoria Bridge, over a variety of gradients. A quarter of a mile at 1 in 170, slackened to a gentle 1 in 1440 for just over a third of a mile. Two short falls at 1 in 40, separated by a furlong at 1 in 79, brought the tram to Fyfin halt. There was no loop at Fyfin, since there was no local industry that required wagons to be left for traffic purposes. There was an isolated post office at a side road, and a few houses half a mile away beside the road in a southerly direction.

Entered on a two chain curve, and a quarter of a mile beyond Fyfin, the line met its most formidable downgrade, falling at 1 in 34 for half a mile. At this point the tramway ran on the northern slope of the Liscreevaghan Burn, a streamlet that tumbled towards its confluence with the River Strule. Two other unstaffed halts, named Stonewalls and Glen,

Crewe 'Station', from the 25" 1907 Ordnance Survey map, sheet Tyrone 16.7 (To scale).

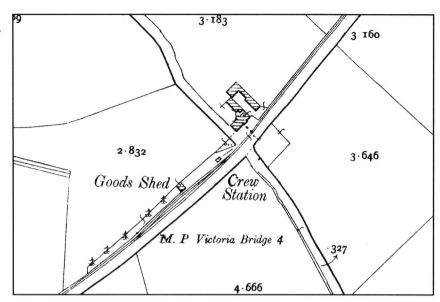

Crewe on 7 August 1930. A cattle train hauled by No 4 sits at Crew loop to await No 5 on the passenger train from Victoria Bridge, seen approaching. The cattle train was occasioned by the Friday fair at Castlederg and was running late. As the line was not signalled it was highly unusual for two trains to meet.
H C Casserley, courtesy M Pollard.

were sited along this final mile of the the tramway. It seems doubtful that these halts were open simultaneously, since neither is shown in 'Bradshaw'. Glen halt appears to have been put into use about 1912-13.

The 1 in 24 downgrade led to Victoria Bridge yard and was steep enough to give the train crew some cause for care, when working in either direction. It ended in a curve of 132 feet (2 chains) radius (120 ft according to Newham [5]) turning into the Victoria Bridge yard and ending at the back of the Great Northern down platform. Some of the curve was on

This cattle train, probably a Fair Day special, has stopped at the top of the steep decent into Victoria Bridge, probably to pin down the brakes. Fireman Robert Irwin poses against the engine, while his driver looks on. The train engine is No 4. The view is looking west.

H C Casserley

level ground and it terminated in seven yards of straight track.

The working practice here is of interest. On entering Victoria Bridge, a train drew to a halt on the 1 in 34 and was held on the handbrake. The engine was uncoupled and went ahead, turned into a short siding and stopped clear of the main line. The points were reset and, controlling the train by the handbrake, the guard allowed the vehicles to creep down the remainder of the downgrade, around the 2 chain curve and into the platform. The engine then reversed up to the points on the main line, the fireman reset the points, the

Victoria Bridge yard, looking north, with 2-4-0T No 3 heading out for Castlederg. The GNR station-master's house (see rear cover) is on the left and the station building is just visible behind the carriage.

Michael Pollard collection

Two views of the CVBT platform at Victoria Bridge in 1963, showing that little had changed over 30 years, apart from the tracks being lifted.

Left: *Looking south-east towards the GNR level crossing. GNR siding on the right.*
                                    John Langford

Below: *Looking north-west with the former trans-ship shed visible in the distance.*
                                    S J Carse

engine regained the main line and cautiously rejoined its train. It was all a little unorthodox and probably was not authorised by the Board of Trade but it was unattended by accidents, apart from an early breakaway that forced the company to adopt the Westinghouse brake.

The Victoria Bridge yard was shared with the Great Northern Railway. It was furnished with a cattle pen, water tank and a stationary two ton crane. The GNR goods shed contained a trans-shipment platform. Levels of the broad and narrow gauge lines were arranged so that the floors of wagons were at the same height as the platform, making it an easy matter to barrow material across. Cattle were trans-shipped by means of gangways on small wheels, running transversely, and placed opposite to the wagon doors, making it a simple matter to drive the animals from one wagon to another. Coal came into Victoria Bridge

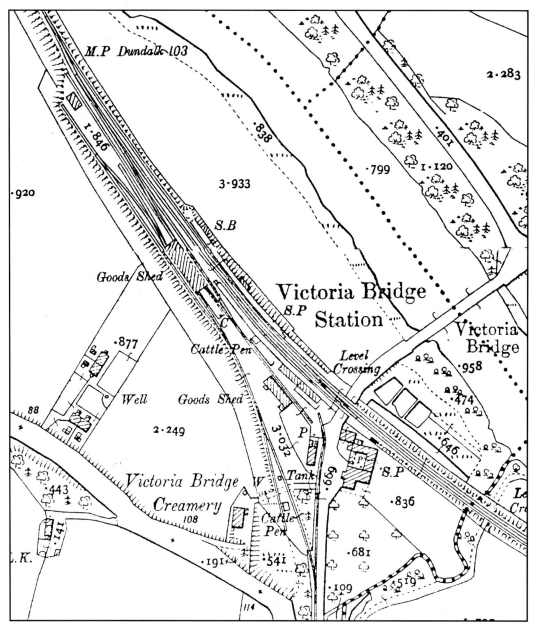

Victoria Bridge station, showing both the CVBT and GNR stations. Notice that a GNR siding came through the trans-shipment shed and terminated adjacent to the CVBT platform. Reproduced from the 25" 1907 Ordnance Survey map, sheets Tyrone 10-9 and 10-13 (to scale).

in Great Northern wagons, these were run onto a section of line at a higher level than the narrow-gauge, and the coal shovelled on to an iron chute whence it fell by gravity into the Castlederg wagon. It was claimed that the cost of trans-shipping goods did not exceed 4d per ton.

The trans-shipment shed and 2 ton crane. Ex GNR lines on the right.
S J Carse, 1963

The tramway was single line, part from the two loops and, since the bulk of traffic was worked under the principle of 'one engine in steam', there was no system of signalling. On rare occasions, such as the monthly cattle fair at Castlederg, two trains were run and crossed at either the Spamount or Crew loop, the operation being prearranged with the engine crews and always taking place in daylight.

The CVBT had no station master of their own at Victoria Bridge but the GNR station master is believed to have attended

No 5 taking water at Victoria Bridge, 21 May 1924.
Ken Nunn Collection, LCGB

to any tramway paper work, before passing documents 'up the line' to Castlederg.

Permanent way on the tramway was of 45lb steel flange rail, which was laid on cross sleepers set 2 ft 6 in apart, though at joints the separation was two feet. The sleepers were of high quality, creosoted Baltic timber six feet in length, and eight inches in width by four inches in thickness, machine-grooved to take the rails. The necessary elevation and cant was given to the outer rail on curves. The rails were nominally 27 ft in length, secured to the sleepers by six ⅝ inch fang bolts, two at each end plus two in the middle, while to the remaining sleepers they were held by a pair of ⅝ inch jagged spikes. the rails were joined by ordinary fish-plates, secured by four Ibbotson's steel bolts and nuts [5].

4

Construction, Opening and Operation

CONSTRUCTION OF THE tramway was a comparatively simple operation, since a good metalled road already existed between Castlederg and Victoria Bridge. It was up to the Grand Jury, predecessor of Tyrone County Council, to lay down the width of the narrowed roadway, which had to be a minimum of 18 feet.

As constructed, the formation level varied from three feet below the road surface to two feet above it. Where rail level was much below the road, the entire width of the road was cut down to rail level and resurfaced. The line was hand-pitched six inches deep for the full width of eight feet and from this to the bottom of the sleepers was four inches of ballast, which was brought up to within two inches of the top of the rails. Where rail level was six inches to one foot above the road surface, a stone kerb was laid alongside the sleeper ends to retain the ballast. When rail level was more than one foot above the roadway, a dry stone retaining wall was built.

This view of a road-side black-smith's forge between Castlederg and Victoria Bridge is of interest because it shows the height of the CVBT track formation in the foreground. This must have been most inconvenient for the occupant. The forge was built in 1641 and owned latterly by four generations of the Monteith family from the Curragh of Kildare. It is said that King James II had his horse shod here by candlelight on his way to the siege of Derry in 1689. The building has since been demolished.

Michael Pollard collection

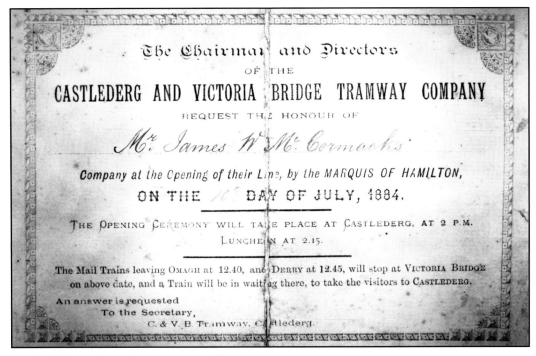

An invitation to the opening ceremony on 10 July 1884.

Where the tramway passed through the two townlands of Craigmonaghan (Nelson) and Craigmonaghan (Funston), about a mile out of Castlederg, it was constructed on the existing footpath and here the company formed a new footpath on the opposite side of the road to route pedestrian traffic away from rail traffic.

Some anxiety soon began to be felt by the directors concerning the steep descent into Victoria Bridge station. A runaway here could have had disastrous consequences, particularly if tramway vehicles fouled the Great Northern main line. Moreover it had been found that obstructions such as loose stones lodged between the running rail and the guard rail might lead to a derailment. Against this, tests had been made in which wagons had been permitted to run loose down the gradient, when it was found that their downhill progress could be controlled by their handbrakes. While this may have been comforting, control was certainly dependent on capable staff being in the right place at the right time.

On Saturday 5 July 1884, Major Marindin, of the Board of Trade, made a formal inspection and passed it as fit to operate. Five days later the tramway was officially declared open.

As it was an important occasion locally, the official opening of the tramway was attended with a good measure of pomp and circumstance. The Marquis of Hamilton had agreed to declare the tramway open and is supposed to have made a special journey from far-off England for that purpose, although his Irish residence at Baronscourt was only a few miles away from Castlederg. The invitation card (above) gave details of connecting trains on the Great Northern, and directors and guests assembled at Victoria Bridge in the late morning of 10 July, piled into the 4-wheel carriages and set off up the hill towards Castlederg. According to the local press the journey took 33 minutes and the reporter also noted that any horses that were passed on the way "hardly noticed" the train.

When the cavalcade reached Castlederg, everyone present crowded to the front of the train, where the Marquis smashed a bottle of champagne against the locomotive and declared the line open for traffic. It must have been a splendid and rather exciting occasion for the Castlederg people, certainly something that they had not witnessed before and would never see again. On the invitation of the directors, a party of nearly 200 guests were entertained to a celebration luncheon in the station goods shed which was suitably decorated for the occasion. At the end of the meal, the company chairman William King proposed the loyal toast of Her Majesty Queen Victoria. This was received with great fervour and led to the singing of the National Anthem. The Marquis of Hamilton then proposed "The success of the Castlederg and Victoria Bridge Tramway" and various other toasts followed. The ceremony came to an end with the Chairman toasting "The Ladies".

On the same day as the official opening, the *Derry Sentinel* newspaper carried an advertisement announcing that public services would start on Friday 11 July. An accompanying timetable showed trains leaving Castlederg at 0925, 1410 and 1615, and from Victoria Bridge at 11.25 am, 3.10 pm and 5.15 pm. Calls would be made at Spamount, Crew and Stonewalls. On Fridays only, there was a late train at 6.40 pm from Castlederg, connecting with the 6.30 pm train out of Londonderry. A return working left Victoria Bridge at 7.25 pm. On Castlederg Fair Day, which was on the last Friday of each month, a special

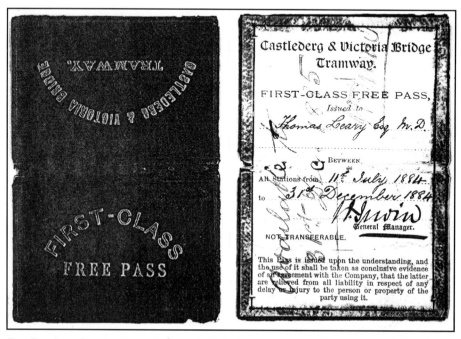

Free Pass issued to Dr Thomas Leary on 11 July 1884.   *Courtesy Tom McDevitte*

goods working for perishable foodstuffs, probably mainly butter and eggs, ran from Castlederg market at 12.10 pm. No service was ever provided on Sundays and there seems to have been little local demand for that. What people never had, they never missed.

The sectional mileage and timings in the Down direction were:

Castlederg to Spamount	1.5	miles	8 min
Spamount to Crew	1.6	miles	16 min
Crew to Fyfin	1.2	miles	7 min
Fyfin to Victoria Bridge	2.8	miles	9 min
Totals with 3 stops:	7.1	miles	40 min

The balance sheet for the first half-year's working (to 31 December 1884) showed a small excess of income over expenditure. Trains had run 9,464 miles; 15,966 passengers and 2,576 tons of goods had been carried. If in this first half year there were 24 weeks each of 6 days, this gives 144 working days. Averaging these figures shows that 68 miles were run each day, 111 passengers travelled each day and 18 tons of goods were carried each day. This was achieved by working 38 trains per week. These were all very modest figures but out of which one is left to wonder how, before the train ran, 55-56 persons managed to get from one end of the line to the other each day, whether by walking, on a bicycle or by horse drawn vehicle, for this total of passenger journeys represents a journey by a 14th part of the entire population of Castlederg. There was clearly little margin for error.

Though the tramway had been cleared by the Board of Trade inspection in early July, it is clear that that august body was by no means satisfied with the Parker-Smith continuous brake that the Castlederg management had fitted to their stock. The directors discussed the matter, from both the safety and economic aspects. In due course the Board of Trade insisted on the provision of efficient continuous brakes. Faced with this unexpected expense at an early stage in the history of the line, the chairman expressed his opinion that the Board of Trade demands were unnecessary and thus exposed some lack of appreciation of such safety matters. It took the terrible Armagh accident of 12 June 1889, four years later, to compel Parliament to pass an Act that made compulsory the fitting of automatic continuous brakes on all railways. The board had already decided to fit their stock with Westinghouse continuous air brakes and placed an order for their supply. The unexpected cost was met through borrowing. Fitment of the Westinghouse equipment imposed heavy demands on the limited workshop facilities at Castlederg and it was not until August 1886 that the Manager, Mr Irwin, was able to publicise it by staging a demonstration to a reporter from the Derry Standard. Though they did not realise it at the time, they were the first company in Ireland to fit Westinghouse brakes.

At the time of the decision to use Westinghouse brakes, it was announced that a contract for carrying mails had been secured, giving a small measure of secure income. In addition, the rates for the transport of livestock had purposely been made very low in order to attract this traffic, previously in the hands of local carriers.

Four and a half miles up river from Castlederg is a hamlet of a few houses which had developed at a junction of four roads. Its name, Killeter, derived from the Irish for a wooded place, and it was about one fifth the size of Castlederg. The Derg valley was broader there, with many small scattered farms. To the south, outliers of the Sperrin mountain range rose to around 1000 feet. It was scarcely promising ground through which to build a railway but, now that the CVBT had become a fact and a landscape feature, the local press reported that the ratepayers of Killeter had held a meeting there on 20 December 1890 "to promote a light railway from Castlederg to Killeter". Euphoria had seized the valley people, but it was unlikely that too many of those small farmers had a clear conception of the capital involved or the other attendant complications. While gradients on the line would have been light, so would the traffic and the profit. Had a civil engineer looked at the ground, a roadside tramway rather than a light railway would have resulted. In the event, nothing more was heard of the Castlederg and Killeter Extension Tramway and it slid away in the shades of local history.

Also in 1891, on 31 July, there occurred a fatal accident to a road user. A man named Kelso was riding on horseback to Castlederg Fair. As a train passed, the animal reared and Kelso was thrown and killed. Several accidents also occurred over the years involving frightened horses, one of which involved a William Woods driving a gig while following a flock at Glenglush. The tram overtook the horse, a large chestnut, which shied and ran in front of the tram and was killed. The gig was destroyed but Wood jumped clear and escaped with his life.

There are reputed to have been a total of ten fatalities, of which five involved men killed on the line. The relevant dates are not known. Joe McKeown fell asleep on the line at Mount Bernard and was beheaded. On another occasion a man named Cowder from Grahamstown, a hamlet a mile north of the Spamount Mills, was killed. Two brothers, Robert and Johnny Campbell, both fell asleep on the line at Knox's glen and were run over. One died immediately, the other died later in hospital. The fifth victim was Robert Galloway, whose death occurred in 1928 when he was killed by the railcar, which was being driven at the time by George Pollard. Pollard arrived at Victoria Bridge, profoundly upset, and said to Robert Porter, the guard "You'll need to drive the train back. I have just killed a man back there."

Some of the accidents apparently involved drunks who were walking their unsteady way home from Castlederg, became drowsy and fell asleep across the line. The company ran a late special on the night of the first day of the County Assizes in Castlederg. The locomotives did not have a powerful headlamp and, in the gloom, the driver was unable to spot a dark figure lying across the rails.

At the date of opening, the Secretary and Manager was William Irwin, whose appointment, at a salary of £160 a year, dated from 17 July 1883. After eleven years at Castlederg, Irwin resigned and went to a similar post at Aughnacloy, on the Clogher Valley Railway, at an improved salary of £250 [7]. Irwin was succeeded at Castlederg by W J Davidson, who remained in charge as Secretary and General Manager until 1928 and as Secretary thereafter.

Charles S Bracegirdle, from the Belfast and Northern Counties Railway, was appointed the first Locomotive Superintendent. With the installation of Westinghouse brakes and work on locomotives Nos 1 and 2, he was busily employed in the primitive workshop at Castlederg. He left in 1900 to better himself with the County Donegal at Stranorlar. His

Left: Charles Stewart Bracegirdle, first Locomotive Superintendent of the Castlederg and Victoria Bridge Tramway. He is seen here with his wife Elizabeth Waugh, daughter of Andrew Waugh, publican and grocer, Main Street, Castlederg. Mr Bracegirdle held the post from 1884 to 1900.

Michael Pollard collection

Above: Mr George H Pollard, Locomotive Superintendent 1917-1934, photographed with his wife,

Michael Pollard collection

Left: Mr W J Davidson, Secretary and General Manager 1894-1928, and secretary 1928-34. He is pictured here in Masonic regalia.

Michael Pollard collection

successor was Richard S Smith, who remained for only four years. Smith was followed by W H Holman from 1904 until March 1917. Holman reappeared as fitter-in-charge, still on the narrow gauge, on the Londonderry and Lough Swilly Railway in November 1918 but remained only until January 1919. Thereafter, he is lost sight of. George H Pollard followed Holman in 1917 and remained in office until the line was closed sixteen years later.

George Pollard had considerable musical talents and he became the organist in Castlederg Parish Church. As the local mechanical genius, he was persuaded to construct a pump to provide a compressed air supply for the church organ. It is said that the petrol engine powering the pump made almost as much noise as the organ itself. While an electric drive would have been more tranquil, electric power generation in Castlederg, at 1s 4d (7p) a unit at that time, was in the hands of a private supplier and since the tramway itself was unable to afford electric power in their workshops on the grounds of cost, Mr Pollard would hardly have promoted it for his church work.

In 1919 the 25 year Baronial Guarantee on £13,000 of shares ended, these shares thereafter ranking as ordinaries. In the same year there was a serious local water shortage in Castlederg. Unwisely, the local council resolved to cut the domestic mains supply to the tramway. The directors decided to become independent of the town supply and requisitioned the services of a water diviner. That worthy found indications of sub-surface water behind the engine-shed. A well, thirty feet in depth, was sunk into the underlying sandstone rock and a copious supply of water was found. Thereafter, the square tank, set high on a stone tower in front of the running shed doorways, was no longer filled from the public supply mains and the company was saved further payments for it.

5

Competition from the Roads

T HE LATER YEARS of the First World War passed the tramway lightly by. Little military traffic troubled the line, indeed war conditions created a very heavy traffic in potatoes and the farmers were glad to get them away swiftly to the city markets. The war, however, presaged profound changes in the way that people travelled, changes that did not favour the railways. From possessing a near monopoly, when peace returned the railways found themselves challenged by the internal combustion engines of lorries and private cars.

By 1922, gross receipts were £7348 and expenditure totalled £7180, giving slim net receipts of £168. Under the Settlement of Claims Act 1921, a windfall payment arrived from the government. A bulk payment of £13M was paid to the railways of the UK. The Castlederg Tramway received a once for all payment of £1912. This, with a miscellaneous payment of £7, contributed to a total net income for 1922 of £2087.

Interest, rentals and other fixed charges yielded £230. It was decided to put £1912 to reserve, leaving a balance for dividend on the ordinary shares of £1326, while a similar amount was carried forward to the next account. The future was indeed gloomy, as the pressure of the petrol motor was inexorable.

Competitive road omnibus services first became established in the winter of 1926-27 when C H Donaghy of Omagh began a service between Castlederg, Drumquin and Omagh. However, his market research seems to have been defective and patronage was poor, so he changed his route to Omagh — Victoria Bridge — Strabane. On that more populous route he was more successful and by November 1927 was providing four double workings a week between Omagh and Derry, plus four additional runs between Strabane and Derry. These were in competition with the Great Northern rather than with the Castlederg tram.

D R Roberts of Derry, who had opened the first bus service in the North West in 1912, began to run a bus between Strabane, Sion Mills, Victoria Bridge and Castlederg on 1 October 1926. He initially provided three double workings, two of which extended to Killeter. The Great Northern Railway saw that Roberts was in direct competition with themselves and bought Roberts out, paying him £4300 for the six buses involved. The purchase gave the GNR an entry into Derry from Stranorlar and the service was later extended towards Donegal, Ballyshannon and Sligo.

Two services, based in Omagh, were operated by William A Simpson and Mrs Margaret Charlton. The first of these was between Omagh and Enniskillen, commencing in November 1928, through Great Northern territory. A year later they reopened the Omagh-

Although of poorer photographic quality than we would normally publish, this view at Victoria Bridge is of considerable interest in showing a light blue Dennis bus operated by D R Roberts of Londonderry, driven by George Martin. This is also the only known photograph of a train sitting at the CVBT platform in Victoria Bridge. The engine is the ex-NCC Beyer Peacock 2-4-0T.

Tom Mc Devitte collection

Drumquin-Castlederg route, which traversed a thinly populated area, where C H Donaghy had unsuccessfully attempted to run buses in 1926. Simpson wisely started the service on a bi-weekly basis, with buses making two double workings on Thursdays and on Saturdays. By 1934 with the Castlederg Tramway out of the way, he began a daily through working from Castlederg to Enniskillen via Omagh. The bus left Castlederg at 1030 and was due in Enniskillen at 1245, whence it departed on its return run at 1415. Eventually, the Northern Ireland Road Transport Board took over the route and paid the owner £8500 for the five buses. In these ways and on these routes, road transport provided the Tyrone public with a better service than the tramway had been able to do.

6

From Hand to Mouth

WHEN MR DAVIDSON took over management in 1894, he found that the system had been allowed to run down and that repairs to the track, mainly involving re-sleepering ·and attention to the rolling stock, were necessary. The directors accepted his verdict and set the cost against revenue during the following two years.

Even as early in 1903, revenue was down on former years, since current low market prices for stock has caused farmers in the area to wait 'for better times' and to hesitate to send their beasts to market, letting them fatten in their fields instead. Added to which, the independent cartage of goods by local carriers was extending. Management were asked by the board to negotiate with the Great Northern and with merchants in an attempt to combat this competition. To provide a better service, new wagons were purchased from Oldbury in 1890 and again in 1899 and, to stimulate traffic indirectly, merchants' tickets for weekly visits were placed on offer.

After twenty years work, the original pair of Kitson engines had become worn out and, since one of them had met with a minor accident, it was resolved that rather than spend precious money on repairs, it would be wiser to scrap both of them and buy a new and more powerful locomotive. Accordingly an order was placed with Hudswell Clarke and Company for a 2-6-0 tank engine at a cost of £1600. This decision was wise from the traffic aspect, but its purchase burdened the little company financially and resulted in the share holders foregoing a dividend for some years. The new engine was delivered in 1904 but, although heavier trains could be worked, the total weight of the new engine was around 80% greater than the little Kitsons (though the axle load was little different). The Engineer, William Purdon, urged that the re-sleepering programme should be stepped up, since many of the original timbers were decayed.

By 1909 the purchase of a cargo of new sleepers gave a stock sufficient to complete the replacement of the originals. However, the 1883 45lb rails were badly worn, particularly on the curves and, in 1915, steps were taken to obtain heavier section rails in second hand condition. Sixty pound rails, mainly derived from the Sligo, Leitrim and Northern Counties Railway, with about 10% derived from the Great Northern, began to be laid, a gradual process that extended over several years.

In fact, the tramway was fighting for its life in the first twenty years of the new century and it was becoming increasingly obvious that the concern was incapable of withstanding temporary reversals in the local farming economy. An outbreak of foot-and-mouth disease that prevented the movement of cattle was an example of this. There was insufficient

2-6-0T No 4 at Castlederg shed around 1924. The four staff in the photo are James Porter (on the running plate), his brother Robert Porter (conductor), Thomas Sturdy (goods porter) and Thomas Gilloway (engine driver).

Real Photographs X1564

0-4-4T No 5 at Castlederg on 7 August 1930. This mixed train has probably just arrived from Victoria Bridge and is sitting alongside the station building. The crew are Thomas Gilloway (driver) and Robert Irwin (fireman)

H C Casserley 7014

industrial traffic in the Castlederg hinterland to hoist the company over many lean years of agricultural depression. The creation of an inter-state border in 1921 raised problems of customs examination that did nothing to assist survival. Then in 1926 the British coal strike added to the Tramway's troubles by increasing the cost of locomotive coal fivefold.

The Company had already answered the challenge by the only means known to it and, in 1925, George Pollard, the Locomotive Superintendent, assisted by Sam Graham a carpenter, and by a blacksmith called John Doherty, constructed a paraffin-driven railcar (see chapter 9). It was considerably underpowered and rather long in the wheelbase but it allowed them to falter on into 1928, during which period the vehicle covered almost 30,000 miles.

By the end of 1928 the financial position was less acute and it became possible to revert to steam traction with mixed trains. Unfortunately, by this time the No 3 Kitson was so worn out after 37 years work that its replacement was necessary. At the end of 1927 it had been cobbled together at a cost of £28.18p, involving the application of a patch on the firebox, plus the insertion of some secondhand steel tubes into the boiler. Tested to a pressure of 150lbs/sq in, it worked traffic through the winter, from 29 November 1927 until May 1928. It was then condemned by the Castlederg management and, after some delay, it was finally sold for £50 in December 1928 and scrapped. For a several months after the demise of No 3, only the two Hudswell Clarke engines — Nos 4 and 5 — were available to keep traffic moving, until the arrival of ex-NCC No 105, which entered traffic in March 1929.

7

The Closing Years

B Y 1932 THE fortunes of the little railway, which had never been a prosperous concern, were markedly on the decline though road competition [6], not the least of which were the operation of buses, and lorries carrying livestock. Even at this time the Government of Northern Ireland was bent on closing as many of the railways as possible and replacing them with road transport. The final nail in the Castlederg's coffin was a strike which lasted from 31 January to 8 April 1933. This affected the CVBT and also the Great Northern, and the LMS (NCC), but not the Belfast and County Down. On 30 September a Special Meeting of the directors and shareholders was called and the Company was wound up, W J Davidson being appointed Official Liquidator.

The position over these last years is summarised in the table opposite, which is abstracted from the last Annual Report.

This photograph is from a postcard titled "Castlederg Roadside Tramway (1883-1933)" and may well be a record of the last weeks of operation. The engine is the ex-NCC 2-4-0T which, with brake van No 2 and presumably a train, is bound for Victoria Bridge. The men in this photograph are (left to right) John Donaldson, clerk at Spamount Mills; Robert Porter, guard; Robert Foye, son of the Ardstraw School Master, who frequently raced the tram on his bicycle (and often won!); John Fox, fireman and Thomas Gilloway, driver.

E M Patterson collection

Summary of Financial Results 1925-1932

	1925	1926	1927	1928	1929	1930	1931	1932
	£	£	£	£	£	£	£	£
Total Expenditure on Capital Account (No.4)	25,122	25,122	25,122	25,122	25,122	25,122	25,122	25,122
Gross Receipts from businesses carried on by the Company (No.8)	4,499	3,805	3,957	4,273	3,750	2,619	2,778	2,166
Revenue Expenditure on ditto (No.8)	4,900	4,233	3,959	5,520	4,426	3,874	3,401	3,192
Net Receipts on ditto (No.8)	- 401	- 428	- 2	- 1,247	- 676	- 1,255	- 623	- 1,026
Miscellaneous Receipts (Net) (No.8)	665	21	8	7	15	10	11	12
Total Net Income (No.8)	264	- 407	6	- 1,240	- 661	- 1,245	- 612	- 1,014
Interest, Rentals,and other Fixed Charges (No.9)	230	233	229	260	—	—	—	—
Dividends on Guaranteed and Preference Stocks (No.9)	—	—	—	—	—	—	—	—
Balance after payment of Preference Dividends (No.9)	34	- 640	- 223	- 1,500	- 661	- 1,245	- 612	- 1,014
Dividend on Ordinary Stock (No.9)	—	—	—	—	—	—	—	—
Rate per cent.	—	—	—	—	—	—	—	—
Surplus (+), Deficit(-)	+34	- 640	- 223	-1,500	- 661	- 1,245	- 612	-1,014
Appropriation from Reserve	—	261	239	—	—	—	—	—
Brought forward from previous years	699	733	354	370	- 1,130	- 1,791	- 3,036	- 3,648
Carried forward to subsequent years	733	354	370	- 1,130	- 1,791	- 3,036	- 3,648	- 4,662

Following the closure of the Tramway, the assets of the Company were disposed of. Locomotive No 4 was purchased by the Clogher Valley Railway and was transported by GNR wagon to Maguiresbridge (see Chapter 8). The CVR also purchased a number of CVBT wagons. Other rolling stock was scrapped or sold, some carriages ending up as hen houses. This led to the discovery of carriage No 4 in 1990 and its subsequent recovery and restoration by the Ulster Folk and Transport Museum. Engine No 5 was used on the lifting train and the following selection of photographs, taken in the second half of 1934, show the lifting gang and No 5 at work.

Castlederg and Victoria Bridge Tramway staff posed outside the works at Castlederg in 1934. From the left they are Thomas Gilloway, Thomas Sturdee, Mr Todd (with hat), ? Sproule, Robert Porter, John Fox (?),W Patrick, Robert Irwin, Mr Pollard and J Porter (?).

Michael Pollard collection

Lifting train at Spamount, 27 July 1934. This view allows us to see inside one of the CVBT brake vans.

No 5 shunting wagons at Victoria Bridge. Note the stacks of recovered sleepers.

Michael Pollard collection

Another view of the lifting train at Spamount.

Rev W A McCourt

Castlederg and Victoria Bridge Tramway wagons at Aughnacloy (Clogher Valley Railway) 13 May 1937. Included are Nos 25, 4 and 22 and at least ten others.

R G Jarvis

Mr Robert Porter with a former CVBT brake van at Castlederg in the 1970s.
Michael Pollard collection

CVBT carriage No 4 under restoration at the Ulster Folk and Transport Museum, 1992.
Michael Pollard

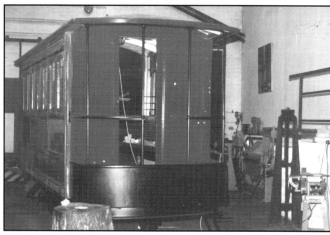

8

The Steam Locomotives

A S THE CONSTRUCTION of the line neared completion, the directors had to decide what motive power to order. At this stage it seemed likely that the line was to be worked on the principle of one engine in steam, so that the minimum requirement would be for two engines. In the event, it was found possible to operate the line with a pair of engines from 1884 until 1892.

In the absence of information from the Board minute books, it is not now possible to determine whether at this stage a number of locomotive manufacturers were canvassed. The directors were local businessmen and had little practical experience to guide them. Although railways had operated in Ireland for over 50 years they were, for the most part, on the Irish standard gauge of 5'3", and narrow gauge lines had only a limited history to draw upon.

At the date of the Castlederg's conception only four narrow gauge lines had commenced to work. Two of these were in County Antrim — the Ballymena, Cushendall and Red Bay Railway and the Ballymena and Larne Railway. Both of these had evolved in response to mining of bedded iron-ore in the Antrim Plateau and were primarily mineral lines with subordinate passenger workings. Their gradients, though long and arduous, never reached the steepness of the Castlederg's 1 in 30. Furthermore, they were several times the length of the Castlederg. The other two lines had more in common with the Castlederg. The Portstewart Tramway, also in Co Antrim, was a short roadside line of 1¾ miles, from a seaside town to the nearest standard gauge railway station at Cromore. Its gradient plan has never been published but the author recalls, as a small boy, on a shopping expedition to Henry's shop across the road from the harbour, listening to the flange-squealing entry of the engine into the 50 yard ascent from the esplanade to the first passing loop at Victoria Terrace, up a formidable gradient that has been measured as 1 in 17. The fourth of these early lines was the Dublin and Lucan Tramway, its length of 6¾ miles practically the same as the Castlederg and having fearsome gradients out of the Liffey River valley with portions of 1 in 20. Certainly the operating problems of the Lucan tram were not dissimilar to those of the Castlederg, with the Portstewart a close second. Neither line accepted mineral or livestock traffic, and had no open wagons. Portstewart and Lucan had both gone to Kitson and Co for their tramway engines and were getting satisfactory work out of them.

Nos 1 & 2, Kitson 0-4-0WT 1883

Kitson & Co were marketing various types of tramway engine, differing essentially in cylinder dimensions and boiler size. Their first steam tram engine was built for the Leeds Tramway Co in 1880. Though there were several other builders of steam tram engines, the Kitson design was soundly engineered and was proving very successful, over 300 being marketed between 1879 and 1901. The original Leeds engine was powered by 2 cylinders of 7″ bore and 12″ stroke, fitted with a modified Walschaerts valve gear. To avoid alarming passing horses, an air cooled condenser of 252 tubes was placed on the roof the the engine. Wheels and motion were hidden from view by steel skirting to within a few inches of rail level.

In addition to differences in gauge ranging from 3′0″ to 4′8½″, Kitson were offering customers four variants of their standard engine. They were:

Type	Cyls	Wheel dia	Tank Capacity	Weight loaded	Wheelbase
1	7¼″ x 12″	2′4¾″	80 gall	7½ tons	4′6″
2	8½″ x 12″	2′4¾″	170 gall	9 tons	
3	9 ″ x 15″	2′9″	455 gall	10½ tons	
4	11½″ x 15″	2′9″	250 gall	13½ tons	6′6″

The wheelbase was influenced by boiler length. The makers' class name was derived from the number of panels or windows along each side. For instance, the lighter Portstewart engine had four panels, a heavier version was styled 'Five panel', whilst the muscular Castlederg engines were 'Six panel heavy class' in the case of Nos 1 and 2, and 'Six panel heavy improved class' in the case of the later No 3.

Nos 1 and 2 bore makers' Nos T 106 and T 107, were named *Mourne* and *Derg* for a short time and served the tramway until developing traffic demand a third engine in 1891. Cylinder sizes of all three were somewhat larger than the sizes given in the above table, and were 12″x15″. The 12″x18″ given by Newham [5] is in error. The boiler pressure was 160 psi. The first pair of engines were completely enclosed, including the boiler, resembling a garden shed on wheels. Engines Nos 1 and 2 carried 318 gallons of water, held in two well tanks. A few years after the delivery of No 3, Nos 1 and 2 were remodelled at Castlederg, under C S Bracegirdle's supervision, roof and side windows being cut away, while modifications were made to the condensing mechanism. The tractive effort of Nos 1 and 2 was 8860 lb at 85% bp.

This is the only known picture of the either of the first two CVBT locomotives. It is not clear if this builder's picture is of No 1 or No 2. Notice the six window panels referred to opposite.

Brian McDaid collection

No 3, Kitson 0-4-0WT 1891

Before No 3 (M No 257) was delivered, the onerous Board of Trade restrictions were

Castlederg and Victoria Bridge Tramway No 3 at Castlederg. This Kitson was built in 1891 and is seen here largely in original condition with side skirts and the plates hiding the motion still in place.

Michael Pollard collection

eased, and that engine had a normal cab with only the cylinders and motion shrouded. The 'improved' No 3 had three well tanks, holding 455 gallons in total. The boiler pressure of No 3 was reduced to 140 psi, having been 160 psi originally. This reduced the tractive effort from 8860 lb at 85% to 7753 lb.

The later history of No 3 is known from G T Glover's notes. In October 1927, a patch was put on the firebox and some second-hand steel tubes were fitted to the boiler. It was tested to 150 psi and worked traffic from 29 November 1927 to May 1928. By then it was in need of general repairs that would have cost £215 and needed a new firebox estimated at £275, together giving the engine a life of only two years. Scrapping was authorised by Glover in December 1928. Scrap value was reckoned at £25 in October, but in fact twice that sum was realised two months later when it came to be sold. The brake fittings were removed for use on a second-hand engine that came at the time from the NCC.

The heating surface dimensions of No 3 in its final years were: firebox 33.5 sq ft, tubes 235.8 sq ft, giving a total of 269.3 sq ft. There were 96 tubes of 1¾" diameter. Grate area was 7.3 sq ft. The bunker held 22 cubic feet of coal.

Published dates of withdrawal of these three tramway engines vary rather widely. In 1931 Henry Casserley gave "about 1900" for Nos 1 and 2. Kidner [7] gave 1904 for both engines, whilst Fayle in 1946 [8] had "probably 1904" for No 1 and "1912" for No 2. Fayle's dates are likely to be the most accurate, since they correspond to the acquisition dates of new engines and these withdrawal dates would have maintained the working stock at the requisite three engines.

No 3 on 20 May 1924. In this view the plates hiding the Walschaerts valve gear have been removed and one of the hinged flaps over the driving wheels has also gone.

Ken Nunn collection 3932, LCGB

No 3 again, possibly in final condition, seen here with neither hinged flap and sitting on the old turntable outside Castlederg shed. Note the large counter-weights on the wheels.

Michael Pollard collection

No.4, Hudswell Clarke 2-4-0T 1904

The new engine that came in 1904 was ordered from Hudswell Clarke. It bore the makers' number 698. It is not known whether it was ordered on the recommendation of R S Smith, who left Castlederg that year, or of his replacement, W H Holman. It was a powerful 2-6-0 side tank. A makers' photograph, taken before the wheel valance was fitted, shows it with the name *Victoria* on the tanks but this name does not appear to have been adopted in service. The cost of the engine, £1600, deprived shareholders of dividends for several years.

Hudswell Clarke photograph of No 4 as built, with temporary nameplate. Skirts not yet fitted.

Courtesy P Mallon

Driving wheels were 3′1″ in diameter, set at 3′4″ and 3′8″ centres, giving a rigid wheelbase of 7′0″ which was about as much as the Victoria Bridge curve could suffer. Cylinders were outside, 13½″x18″. Boiler centre line was 6′1″ above rail level, its length 9′0″, and diameter 3′3″, working at 160 psi. Tractive effort at 85% bp was 12,058 lb, an increase of around 50% over the old tramway engines. The copper firebox was 3′2″ in length inside, 1′10″ wide at the top and 2′10″ at bottom, while its height was 3′11″ and 3′7″ at front and back. Heating surface measurements were; firebox 54 sq ft, tubes 542.4 sq ft, on the outside of 120 tubes of 1¾ diam. The tubes were originally brass but were replaced, first by Armco iron and in 1928 by secondhand steel tubes. In an effort to give the engine capability in negotiating curves, the overall wheelbase of 11′0″ resulted in a long overhang at front and rear.

The engine was "fitted with steam condensing gear" [18], but at some unknown date this was removed. When the GNR assumed supervision in 1927, the boiler was taken to

Dundalk and was given a boiler test with 250 lb of water and 180 lb of steam, after the fitting of a new smokebox tube plate, patching of the firebox and fitting of new stays. The work cost £288 11s 5d. The helical spring arrangement was modified, and a pair of trailing laminated springs were substituted behind the rear driving axle. In September 1928 a 2″ long crack was found in the frame behind the side tank on the left

Top: No 4 at Castlederg shed, now fitted with skirts over the motion, but only on the left side as the engine faced Castlederg and this was the side next the road.
Dr H A Whitcombe

Left: Castlederg shed, 7 August 1930. Views of the right hand side of CVBT engines are rare as this side was usually in shade. Note the Westinghouse air pump.
H C Casserley

side and this was patched in March-April 1929. The frames were ¾" and the buffer beams 1⅛" contributing to a total weight, empty, of 21 tons, rising to about 25½ tons in working order.

This engine performed very satisfactorily and lasted until the closure. Rolling stock, workshop equipment and rails were then bought by Arnott, Young & Co Ltd, Fullerton Ironworks, Glasgow as

Three views showing No 4 on its way to Maguiresbridge after sale to the CVR.

Top: *At Victoria Bridge waiting to be loaded.*

Centre: *The engine being loaded onto a GNR bogie well wagon.*

Below: *The two cranes that carried out the lift. Presumably the cranes then proceeded to Maguiresbridge for the unloading.*
Michael Pollard collection

scrap. However, before the 2-6-0T engine could be cut up, the manager of the Clogher Valley Railway, D N McClure, realised the potential of this 30 year old engine and exchanged two of their worn out engines, No 1 *Caledon* and No 7 *Blessingbourne* against it. In October 1934, helped by the Great Northern's two breakdown cranes, Castlederg No 4 was moved from Victoria Bridge to Maguiresbridge. There it was steamed and driven to Aughnacloy, the journey making it clear that the valve timing required to be reset.

Since the Clogher Valley workings were to take No 4 much farther from the Aughnacloy coaling plant than from its accustomed runs to Victoria Bridge, an increase in bunker capacity was necessary. Under McClure's direction, the Aughnacloy shops were equal to the rebuild and overhaul. The frames were lengthened to the rear by two feet, accommodating a bunker 2'6" in length that overhung slightly and held 1½ tons of coal. To support the bunker a rear radial truck with solid 2'6" wheels was grafted on, transforming the engine to a 2-6-2T and increasing the weight by 3 tons. The whistle tone of No 4 was higher pitched than the Clogher Valley's deep hoot. When the engine entered service, even cattle grazing in the fields noticed the difference in the sound and, being inquisitive beasts, for a time they galloped towards their nearest gate for a sight of the different thing that was hauling their familiar train.

No 4 at Aughnacloy in 1934 after being rebuilt by the CVR as a 2-6-0T. It remained No 4 on the CVR.
Michael Pollard collection

To commemorate the Aughnacloy rebuild, McClure obtained an oval brass plate, similar in size to the maker's plate, and inscribed 'Rebuilt 1936 Aughnacloy Works' and proudly fixed it to the bunker, level with the Hudswell Clarke plates of 1904. Aughnacloy made several other changes: the old Ramsbottom safety valves were replaced by Ross Pop valves, and the whistle shifted to a position between the safety valves and the front sheet of the cab. The Westinghouse brake was replaced by vacuum brake gear, salvaged from the CVR's *Blessingbourne*. The light Castlederg buffers, link type with pins, were replaced by the hook

No 4 inside Aughnacloy shed on 25 June 1937. Note the large headlamp fitted to the front, and the complete absence of side skirts. Alongside is a standard CVR 0-4-2T. No 4 remained with the CVR until the line closed in 1941.

LGRP 7411

type of CVR stock and their centre line raised by 3″. To improve the running, laminated springs were fitted to all the driving axles. At Castlederg the driving position had been on the left, giving the driver a clear view of the open road. In the rebuild this remained unaltered, making the engine different in that respect from its seven precursors on the Clogher Valley [9].

No 5, Hudswell Clarke 0-4-4T 1912

With the demise of Kitson No 2 around 1912 another new engine was ordered from Hudswell, Clarke and Co to maintain the engine total at three. It seems to have been considered that a 4-coupled engine with a trailing bogie would give more flexibility on curves, and avoid the besetting sin of low-speed derailments. An 0-4-4T was ordered and was delivered in 1912, maker's No 978 and CVBT No 5. It might have been wise if the Castlederg management had talked to their Clogher Valley colleagues on the behaviour of their Hudswell Clarke 0-4-4T No 7, officially named *Blessingbourne* but colloquially referred to by CVR engine crews as "The Oul' Baste". It had been on the Clogher Valley line for five years but was notorious for 'lossing its feet' and had been consigned to a corner of Aughnacloy yard. The same troublesome fault, lack of adhesion, affected the Castlederg's purchase, especially when getting away from Victoria Bridge.

The driving wheels of No 5 were set at 5′6″ centres and their diameter was 3′1″. The bogie wheels had a diameter of 2′0½″, set at 3′9″ centres, with the leading bogie axle 4′11″ behind the second driving axle. The weight distribution on the four axles is not known and a direct comparison with CVR No 7 cannot be made. Possibly the CVR's trouble was known to the Castlederg board, for the engine arrived with two massive cylindrical sandboxes, resembling a pair of large saucepans, set fore and aft of the steam dome. Their operating levers were linked to a rod that was worked from the cab.

The outside cylinders were 12½″x18″, and the valve gear was Stephenson. The total heating surface amounted to 508.7 sq ft, made up of 48.7 sq ft firebox and 460 sq ft in the 102x1¾″ diameter tubes. Boiler pressure was 160 psi, giving a tractive effort of 10,388 lbs. Grate area was 9 sq ft. The weight empty was 20½ tons, 24½ tons in working order. The side tanks held 510 gallons. The rear bunker held 35 cubic feet of coal.

No 5 had a copper firebox 3′3″ in length inside, 2′9⅞″ wide at the top and 2′11″ at the bottom. Its height was 3′11½″ at both front and back. The driving wheel journals were 7½″x5¼″ diam, and bogie journals were 7″x4¼″.

Once the Castlederg engines came under Great Northern surveillance, a heavy repair to No 5 was ordered in December 1927 and was largely performed at Castlederg. Since there was no wheel lathe at Castlederg, the tyres were turned at Stranorlar. No 5 went back into service in January 1928. It was taken off again for boiler and firebox repairs in June 1929. A copper liner was fitted to the firehole ring and all rivets were renewed in the same. Twenty two copper stays were renewed and 16 rivets and 6 studs were replaced in the foundation ring. A new half front was fitted to the smokebox and the boiler was given a set of secondhand steel tubes, the earlier tubes having been of brass. In November 1929, the left leading tyre was found to be broken and it was replaced by a secondhand old GNR bogie tyre. After these repairs No 5 worked until the tramway closed, and it was then sold for scrap.

Above: Makers' photograph of No 5 showing it as named 'Castlederg'. Note the two sand boxes on the boiler. Side skirts not yet fitted.

Left: No 5 at Victoria Bridge yard on 6 August 1930. Note the side skirts and the air reservoir below the running plate. The long lever emerging from the cab operated the sanding gear.
H C Casserley 7016B

No 5 at Castlederg shed in 1932 with No 4 behind it. Note the spark arrester on the chimney. The hook type centre buffer coupling is clearly visible on both engines. The crew are Thomas Gilloway (left) and Robert Irwin.   *LGRP 6603*

No 5 sets off from Castlederg on the 0815 to Victoria Bridge, 21 May 1924.
     Ken Nunn collection 3934, LCGB

No 3, Beyer Peacock 2-4-0T, second hand 1928

In November 1928 the Castlederg bought one of the original engines of the old Ballymena and Larne Railway, a Beyer Peacock 2-4-0T, that had been built in 1878 [8]. It had been No 4 on the B&LR, but when that company became a part of the Belfast and Northern Counties Railway in 1889 it became No 64. In 1897, all the 3 foot gauge stock of the BNCR was renumbered from 101 upwards and 64 became 105 [10]. It had 12½"x18' cylinders, originally 11"x18", and Allan straight link motion. It passed to the London, Midland and Scottish Railway (NCC) in 1923 and during 1926 spent a short time working on the Ballycastle line. The Northern Counties company had standardised on compound narrow gauge engines and the elderly Beyer engine became surplus to requirements. Accordingly it was declared redundant and was sold for £225 'on wagon at Antrim'.

Its original bell-mouth dome survived into Castlederg ownership. Its driving wheels on the side next the road were protected by an open metal framework, an indignity that it never had to suffer in County Antrim. Although this engine is often described as No 6, it actually displayed no number, and was identified only by the Castlederg crest on its tanksides. In the Castlederg Diagram Book it is described as 'No 3', which was logical, since it was a replacement for the third Hunslet. It arrived at Victoria Bridge on 20 November 1928. It was tested as a light engine on 23 November and derailed on the Victoria Bridge station curve, repeating that feat a week later at the water column. It recovered face by successfully restarting four wagons, two of which were loaded, on the 1 in 34 gradient.

It was then taken to the Castlederg shops where the vacuum brake was replaced by Westinghouse, the couplings altered in height, the cab-side sheet and skirt were fitted, and it went into regular service in March 1929. After five months experience it was found to save 11 cwt of coal per day, compared with No 5. In the following year the Rowan pistons were removed and replaced with a solid version. The engine gave good service on the Castlederg road over the five years that it ran there.

The offside skirts which covered the wheels and motion of the engines, and some of the rolling stock, were intended to avoid alarming horses and possibly discouraging suicidal dogs. They consisted of a sheet of metal that extended from front to rear. In this sheet there were secondary rectangular doors, hinged on the top edge and affording access to the valve gear and bearings for periodic lubrication by the 'long feeder'. On the ex-Ballymena and Larne engine the overall sheet was replaced by an open framework of steel straps, as already mentioned.

Liveries

The livery of engines 1-3 was black, at least latterly. The earliest photograph of No 3 shows the engine to be in a coloured livery, with quite elaborate lining and the side skirts appear a different shade from the engine. Engines 4 and 5 were brick red. Lining consisted of an outer ½" in vermilion and an inner ¼" in yellow. The Beyer engine is not believed to have been repainted after delivery and presumably retained the crimson lake colour of the NCC.

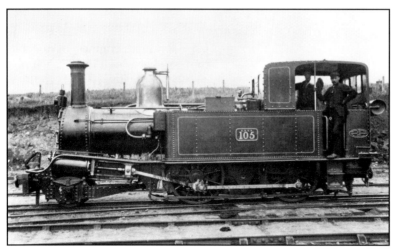

The Beyer 2-4-0T running as NCC No 105. This classic design was first built by Beyer Peacock for the Norwegian State Railways in 1868. More Norwegian examples followed and 13 in various sizes were built for the Isle of Man Railways from 1873 on. Two were built for the BNCR in 1877-8. Note the front Bissel truck.

E M Patterson collection

The same engine as running on the CVBT, seen here at Castlederg on 7 August 1930. The locomotive carried no number in CVBT days, though the Dundalk diagram book identifies it as 'No 3'. Most publications refer to it as 'No 6', though there is no documentary evidence for this. Note the cut out in the cab side sheet, and the frame over the wheels. No photographs show any sheeting on this frame.

H C Casserley 7024

This unusual view of the NCC engine shows that the air reservoir was placed behind the cab, and the Westinghouse pump in the usual position on the side of the smokebox. There was no cut out on the right hand side of the cab. Presumably the driver only needed to observe the road side! Note wagon No 15.

J H Houston, E M Patterson collection

This view looking along Castlederg platform shows engine No 3, coach No 5 and a brake van.

E M Patterson collection

9

The Paraffin-Engined Railcar

INEVITABLY, THE CASTLEDERG management turned their attention to the use of the internal combustion engine as a means of achieving cheaper motive power. The Donegal Railways had been running a paraffin-powered railcar since 1907, mainly for inspection work. Later when a more powerful petrol engine had been fitted, it was used for passenger work as well. Their use of this vehicle had not been lost on the Castlederg management. The Directors decided to acquire one and obtained a quotation from an English company. However, George H Pollard convinced the Directors that he could build it more cheaply. So, assisted by a blacksmith, John Doherty and by a carpenter, Sam Graham, he built a paraffin-driven railcar in the Castlederg workshops. It the event, it cost more to build than the quotation obtained by the Directors! It was powered by a 20 hp Fordson tractor engine driving all four wheels by chains and it could be driven from either end. It was

The railcar when new, with CVBT officials, including Mr Pollard, posing beside it. It is standing outside Victoria Bridge station. Note the cow catcher and the heavily laden hand trolley. Under the engine there was a pony truck with 8" side play.

Reproduced from 'The Locomotive' 15 April 1931

underpowered and was never completely satisfactory but it gave the company a cheaper form of transport than they could ever have had with steam haulage. It worked away for three years, covering 30,000 miles.

Its wheelbase was 17'6", from the front pony wheels to the rear pair of driving wheels. Axle loading was 1T+4½T+4½T giving a total weight of 10 tons. The diagram gives the false impression that there was a second pair of carrying wheels. These are drawn in red in the original and may indicate a proposal for a bogie truck. Though it was underpowered, it was capable of 30 mph, a fact reflected by the November 1927 timetable in Bradshaw, when stopping runs were given as 30 minutes, and the express leaving Castlederg at 7.15 am was into Victoria Bridge at 7.40 am. The wheelbase proved rather too long for the curves, particularly the left hander into the Victoria Bridge yard but the General Manager commented of it that, "when running normally it never left the rails". The drive from the engine was taken through a four-speed forward and reverse gearbox, which was supplied by Rex Transmissions. Double two inch chains conveyed the power to the leading pair of driving wheels, while a central single chain carried the drive to the rear driving wheels. With four-wheel drive, there was no slip even on a wet rail and no sand was ever used.

The body of the railcar was faced with tongue and groove wood, laid vertically. It had the shape of an oblong box, with a slight chamfer fore and aft. Body length was 19'3", and width 6'0". It had two entrances, a single hinged door leading into a tiny porch on the south side of the front driving position. A cross panel divided the body interior into two areas, that in front being slightly longer than the rear. The second entrance was on the south side of the body, just aft of the cross panel, and consisted of double hinged doors, opening outwards. Parcels up to a total weight of 15cwt were stowed on the floor of the rear compartment. There were three wooden bench seats in the front compartment area, two of which were longitudinal, while the third was positioned transversely against the leading side of the cross panel. A further longitudinal bench seat was on the north side of the rear compartment. There were two driving seats, one at each end of the car, and one-man operation by a conductor was practicable, the tickets being issued by him. Twenty passengers were accommodated on seats and eight more standing passengers could be fitted in. According to a letter written by Robert Porter, who drove it, the engine of the railcar was towards Castlederg, as shown on page 57. In the other direction the railcar reversed and, for the passengers, this was more pleasant, because in forward gear the fumes came into the passenger compartment.

Skefko double roller bearings were fitted to the driving axles and ball bearings on the pony truck. Spiral bearing springs were fitted on top of the axleboxes.

In March 1928 the railcar was condemned by George Pollard in a report to the Castlederg directors. It was noted that it consumed 50 gallons of paraffin per week, and the conductor's wage was 48 to 52 shillings per week. In December of that year the board authorised the car to be scrapped and converted into a light van. In fact that was not done. After withdrawal it lay derelict in the open, behind the running shed at Castlederg. On 13 December 1932 Inspector Henry removed the carburettor and magnet as an anti-vandal measure. During September 1929 the engine was taken out of the railcar and sold to the owner of a local sawmill. By December Glover noted that the "coach was lying in shed" where what remained of it was at least under cover from the weather.

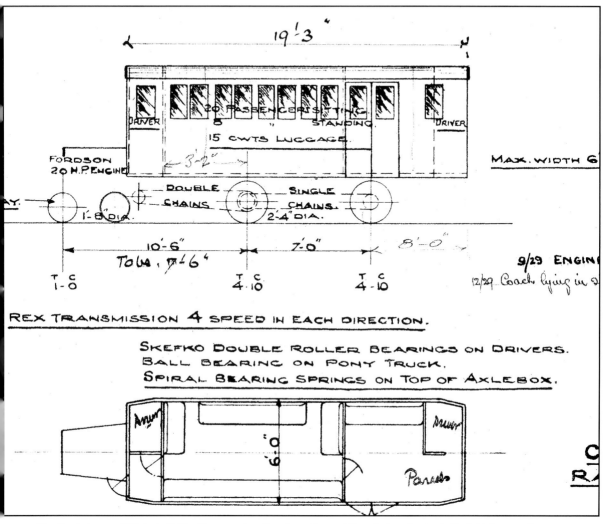

The Castlederg and Victoria Bridge Tramway's railcar from George Glover's drawing book. Scale ³⁄₁₆ " to one foot. Note that the railcar had only one pair of carrying wheels at the front. The second pair were never added.

Courtesy P Mallon

Thus the first excursion of the Tramway company into internal-combustion engined traction lasted from 1924 to Christmas 1928, covering a particularly difficult period in the Tramway's financial history caused, on the one hand, by the British coal strike and, on the other hand, by competition from road omnibuses. The construction and operations of the railcar was in fact a very courageous pioneering trial on the part of a tiny company that had neither experience to guide them, nor a well-equipped workshop. In fact, the inventive George Pollard and his two tradesmen beavered away in an unheated and ill-lit shed that was little different from the traditional village blacksmith's shop.

The CVBT railcar lying derelict at Castlederg in August 1930. The paraffin engine had been removed for sale to a local sawmill in September 1929. H C Casserley 7021

This view of the railcar shows the opposite end to that shown above. It also shows the tongue and grove boarding to good effect. As the engine has been removed, this view was probably taken at Stranorlar in 1933, after the railcar had been purchased by the CDRJC.

Reproduced from the 'Journal of the IRRS', No 25, Vol 5

Three years later, on 15 December 1932, Henry Forbes of the CDRJC, was in Castlederg and viewed the remains of the home-made railcar. Forbes was a traffic man so he referred his thoughts to G T Glover at Dundalk:

"I went today with Mr Armstrong to Castlederg to see the derelict rail motor on hand there. It is certainly not very prepossessing as it lies on the scrap heap; the body is of course quite hopeless but the chassis seems to be in fair order with good wheels and axles, fitted with roller bearings, and I think when fitted with a new body would suit us as a trailer . . . I think a fair offer for would be £25, or £30 on rail at Victoria Bridge station."

The lower figure was offered and brought a plaintive response from W J Davidson:

"I brought your offer for purchase of Coach Body &c before my Directors at their meeting on 19th instant. I was instructed to write you, that while willing to part with the Coach they think the figure offered is too small. It may be of only scrap value while lying here but it will be of very greatly more value to a purchaser to make use of it.
The roller bearings (SKF Co), which are in perfect order on the wheels, cost more than the £25 offered. After all, I think we are entitled to get something more out of the sale, so that this company won't lose all and another company gain all in the transaction."

After some discussion £25 was accepted. Forbes wrote to Glover regarding the deal:

On the Co Donegal Railway the CVBT railcar was given a new body and a Reo petrol engine. It is seen here as CDRJC No 2 at Stranorlar in 1937.

S W Baker

"Mr Davidson's argument is not very logical, viz that while admitting the derelict Motor Coach is of only scrap value to them, the purchaser should pay a fancy price for it, because of some inherent or problematical value it may have that apparently they have failed to discover.
Of course one must make allowance for the pangs of parenthood in a disappointing offspring."

The railcar was towed to Victoria Bridge on 4 January 1933 and was taken, first to Strabane over the GNR and thence to Stranorlar over the CDRJC. It was decided to utilise the vehicle as a railcar rather than a trailer and it was given a six-cylinder Reo FA engine and a new body. As the second No 2 railcar on the Donegal, it had a life of eleven years. By April 1944 it had been lying at Glenties for nearly three years, out of use because of cannibalisation of the engine. It was decided to rebuild it yet again and make it into a trailer, since by then the Donegal had powerful diesel railcars able to tow it. The frame was lengthened by about 3 feet and the seating increased from 16 to 30. As Trailer No 2 it continued in use until the end of 1959, the epitome of the late Henry Forbes' pursuit of economy.

In 1944 the engine was removed from the railcar and it was rebuilt as a trailer. As such it lasted until 1959. It survived as a summer house until quite recently, at St Ernans, Co Donegal.
Michael Pollard collection

10

Diesel Traction

BEFORE THE OPERATION of the home-made railcar had ended, the Castlederg management were contemplating other forms of motor driven traction. In September 1927 Messrs Davidson and Pollard suggested to Dundalk, that a light petrol-driven locomotive with a 50hp Dorman engine and costing £1035, would do their work. The Great Northern vetted the proposal but turned it down. One is driven to the conclusion that Castlederg lacked the technical ability to assess their peculiar local needs. They had been motivated by low capital cost, rather than by the need to haul occasional long stock trains as well as light passenger traffic. Two well established firms, Hudswell, Clarke and Co and J Fowler and Co submitted quotations. These were £2700 and £1965 respectively, both of which figures were more than the Castlederg board could justify.

Events moved slowly but, after two years, interest moved to Kerr, Stuart and Co of Stoke-on-Trent, who submitted a quotation of £1350, and shipped over a 60bhp diesel-

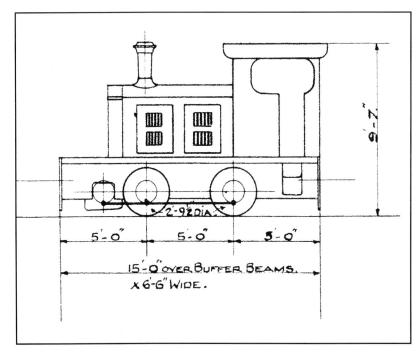

This is the Hudswell, Clarke drawing of the proposed petrol-driven locomotive for the Castlederg line, for which they quoted £2700. It would have had a 50 hp, 6 cylinder Dorman engine, and was Hudswell, Clarke design No 1453. In the event the quotation was too expensive and the locomotive was not built.

Courtesy P Mallon

engined locomotive to Castlederg on trial. It began work on Christmas Day 1929 and worked, or attempted to work, passenger trains. This qualifies the Castlederg and Victoria Bridge Tramway to be the first railway in Ireland to employ diesel traction. The engine was retained until the end of May 1930, a total of 137 days, during which period it was operational for only 70 days, the remainder of the time being laid aside because of a variety of mechanical troubles. A catalogue of such crimes could not be tolerated, even considering the proved saving of £4 per week in fuel and £2 per week in labour costs, compared with a steam locomotive.

Inevitably, Henry Forbes of the Donegal Railways took an interest. He had seen the Atkinson-Walker steam tractor on the Clogher Valley Railway when he had gone there in his capacity as a member of the Committee of Management. Knowing the under-powered defects of the tractor, he wrote to Glover at Dundalk on 17 August 1929:

"I am doubtful if the 60hp diesel would be capable of working our usual mixed train service even over the Ballyshannon branch, at a speed that would enable us to maintain our connections at each end.

We find our new rail motor (40hp) is fairly well taxed to haul at a suitable speed the trailer fully loaded (3 tons) over the moderate banks on the Ballyshannon line, and with one of our ordinary passenger carriages (13 tons) and 2 wagons (10 tons each) behind the Diesel, the speed I fear would be very low if indeed the load could be taken at all. The Castlederg vehicles are much lighter than ours . . . and it might succeed there at 12mph, but this speed would be useless here.

If Mr Stephens and yourself gave us an opportunity of seeing the Diesel working on the Castlederg line, we could very soon form an idea if a trial here would be worth the expense involved, but I am

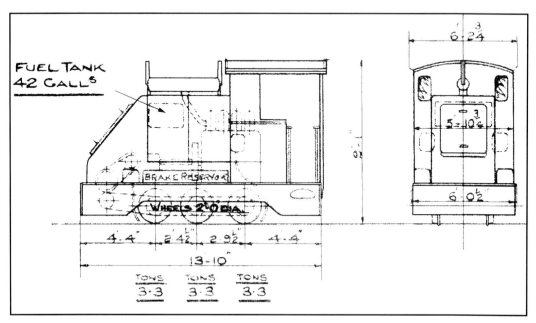

Diagram of the Kerr Stuart diesel locomotive trialed on the Castlederg line between Dec 1929 and May 1930. The scale of both drawings is ⅜" to the foot. Kerr Stuart diagram No 33340. Courtesy P Mallon

disappointed at your suggesting we should disburse £45, half the carriage between Stoke and Castlederg, seeing the loco is being brought over by your Company for a special test at Castlederg.
... I can indeed understand your anxiety to reduce the cost of the test on the Castlederg Tramway to a minimum, but I feel sure Mr Stephens will be generous enough not to insist on our paying the uttermost farthing if we decide to test the Diesel at Stranorlar.

PS It occurs to me we might get the Clogher Valley Railway to give the Diesel a trial, and you could probably get half the rail charges out of them."

Further exchanges of letters took place between Forbes and Glover, the former being obsessed with the idea that a diesel, of whatever power, would be useful on the CDRJC, provided that he could secure it for a bargain price.
Forbes penned a 'Personal' letter on 14 June 1930:

"Dear Mr Glover,
I have just had a visit from Mr Pollard, informing me that they are returning the Diesel to the Makers on Tuesday next, in accordance with your instructions, and as they understood from you, you were disposed to give it a trial on this line, I would be glad to know what you thought of that idea.
I appears the maker would dispose of it for £250 - £300, and we might be able to use it at Strabane for shunting, and perhaps dispense with a run of an ordinary locomotive between here (Stranorlar) and Strabane - What do you think? Or do you consider it would not even be suitable for shunting purposes."

Glover replied on 16 June:

"I cannot recommend you to make a trial with this locomotive, as the troubles with it on the Castlederg Tramway have been so numerous and varied.
It would be most suitable for shunting if it were a reliable Machine, and you may rest assured that, between your investigations and mine, that as soon as a reliable Diesel Machine comes on the market we will investigate its capabilities.
It must be remembered that on the Castlederg Tramway this Engine was employed on the lightest work only, and for the heavy lifts you need at Strabane, it would only cause disappointment.
As this is a personal letter, I would like to say that I entirely acquit Mr Pollard of any want of care or attention in this matter, as I consider he has dealt most fairly with this particular Machine."

Here the matter rested and this was to prove the end of the CVBT experiments with diesel traction.

The performance characteristics of the Kerr Stuart diesel are shown on the accompanying table. It had a 4 cyl 60 bhp McLaren-Benz diesel engine and weighed 10 tons in working order. The engine worked at 800 rpm and had a maximum speed of 11.27 mph

Incline	Top Gear 11.27mph		Bottom Gear 5.8mph	
	@15lbs resistance	@20lbs resistance	@15lbs resistance	@20lbs resistance
	TONS	TONS	TONS	TONS
1in30	13	12	36	34
1in40	20	18	48	45
1in150	61	51	128	109
Level	133	97	268	198

Carriages and Wagons

IN SPITE OF possessing only thirty-six vehicles, the tramway had three separate numbering series; passenger carriages (1-5), brake vans (1 and 2) and goods stock (1 to 29).

For the opening of the line, four passenger carriages came from Oldbury (Railway Carriages Co, Oldbury, Birmingham). All were carried on four wheels and their length over headstocks was 21'0" and over buffers 23'0". As it was soon found that additional carrying capacity was needed, a bogie carriage (No 5) was supplied by Oldbury in 1887. Nos 1 and 2 were first and second class composites. Six first class were confined within a 4'6" section, longitudinally upholstered. The second class had facing slatted wood seats in a 9'6" section, seating seven per side. Carriage No 3 was entirely second class. Its longitudinal seats measured 14'6" and seated a total of 22. Carriage No 4 was for first class travellers and was

Carriage No 1, as built by Oldbury in 1884. In contrast to its eventual condition, note the attractive panelling and the transfers and crest applied directly to the coach sides. In this makers' photograph there are no wire mesh grills on the vehicle.   *Michael Pollard collection*

Carriage No 2 in 1933, after the original lower panelling had been replaced by vertical matchboard material. Note the handbrake, the wire mesh grills and the air brake connection. Two side chains with hooks are fitted, though absent in the view opposite. The first class is marked 'Smoking'. In both this view and the previous one, the curved ends to the carriages and the bow roof can be seen.　　　　　　　　　　　*LGRP 7117*

partitioned into a smoking and a non-smoking section, respectively 8'3" and 6'0" in length and, in theory, seating twenty. The absence of third class accommodation was apparent and, around 1887, the second class was reclassified 'third'. At the same time a new third class bogie carriage, No 5, was built. It measured 33'6" over headstocks and 35'0" over buffers. The seats were placed as in the older vehicles and a cross-partition divided the vehicle into two sections, 12'3" and 14'6". It is possible that one of the sections was for smokers, but no distinguishing label can be seen in a photograph, nor does G T Glover's sketch book provide a statement. Since previous authors have treated details of the rolling stock only briefly, the matter is conjectural.

All five carriages had end verandas which were entered on the off-side (from the roadway) by two steps. To protect passengers from contact with passing brushwood,the four 4-wheelers had wire mesh screens on the near-side of the verandas, extending from floor to roof, while metal sheets were used on the solitary bogie carriage. The roofs, which covered the verandas, had a shallow arched profile with dished ends above the verandas. They were supported on four vertical iron pillars, with a horizontal bar at waist level, with further security being provided by sheet metal toe-boards which were reinforced at the top by a heavy beaded edge. Vertical grab handles were fixed at the corners of the bodywork. Entry to all five carriages was via the end verandas, then through a central sliding door in each body end. Screw hand-brakes were on all verandas on the off-side, so as not to interfere with passenger movements. Photographs show that all the carriage bodies were eventually faced below waist level with tongue and groove boards, laid vertically. However, the earliest photographs show that there was originally attractive panelling on the sides below waist level, at least on the 4-wheelers, and this has been reproduced on the restored No 4. Carriages 1 & 2 had six windows with radiused corners, ranged along each side and each protected by three horizontal iron bars on the inside. The sections between the windows were occupied by recessed panels with half-round extremities. Nos 3 & 4 had seven such windows. On the bogie carriage each side had eleven rectangular-cornered lights, while on the the off-side, four were drop-lights. There were three lights on the carriage ends, facing the verandas.

After the panelling was replaced by match board sides, a wooden disc with the company crest was fixed centrally, while flanking it on the composites were boards carrying 'Third' and 'First' in shaded serifed capitals. Below the crest was the vehicle number. No 5 had the crest alone.

Buffer heights of Irish narrow-gauge stock were notoriously varied, a characteristic which caused difficulties in the latter years when stock was being sold and shifted to other lines. On the Castlederg the central buffer was 1'11in (58.4cm) above rail level. Only the Ballymena and Larne were nearer the ground, at 1ft10½". Although none of the five carriages was reincarnated on another railway, the covered wagons were all bought by the Clogher Valley and are referred to in my book on the CVR [9].

Even though the Castlederg rolling stock did not encounter any overbridges or tunnels, their loading gauge was one of Ireland's smallest [6].

	CVBT	CVR	CDRJC
Overall width of bodywork	6ft 6in (199cm)	7ft 8in	10ft 6in
Height at centre above rails	9ft 6in (290 cm)	11ft 6in	11ft 4in
Height at side above rails	9ft (274cm)	11ft	9ft 6in

On the 4-wheel carriages (Nos 1-4) the protective skirting over the wheels was a rectangle of diagonal mesh wire, edged with heavier rod. It was suspended from the frame of the vehicle and reached to rail level, being steadied by steel bracing straps that extended from the underside of the floor to the lower edge of the skirting. The mesh panel had a length of 14'6", and terminated just short of the access steps. Two openings allowed the grease boxes to project.

On the bogie carriage (No 5) similar diagonal mesh panels were slung but they were in three rectangular sections with lengths measuring 8'0", 10'6" and 8'0". The leading and trailing screens covered each bogie and each had a pair of openings through which the grease boxed projected. The central portion covered the space between the bogies.

Although only four Annual Reports have been available for study, it appears that the percentage of first class seats stood at 26-27%, out of a total of seats amounting to 132. However, based on the percentage of 1st class tickets sold (4.6% in 1919, rising to 6.7% in 1932) it would appear that first class seating was somewhat over-provided. A balancing

Third class bogie carriage No 5. At 35' overall length, this was the largest vehicle in the CVBT fleet. Note the crest and number applied on separate wooden mounts. Gaps were left in the wire mesh for greasing the axle boxes. In contrast to wire mesh on the 4-wheelers, the end balcony on No 5 has solid sheeting on the side next the hedges.   *LGRP 7116*

Scouts leaving Castlederg to head off to camp around 1930. The other youngsters no doubt wish they were going too. Carriage No 5 awaits its engine. Robert Porter has his back to the camera.

Michael Pollard collection

factor may have been season tickets held by commuters. In 1919 these were mainly first class, with a first : third ratio of 10:1. In later years the two classes drew into balance, this occurring in 1923. By 1932 first class season ticket holders had disappeared and only twenty-seven thirds were being requested, bringing in an income of £27.

The two brake vans were numbered 1 and 2 in a separate series. Both came from Oldbury in 1884. Body lengths were 16'0" over headstocks and 18'0" over buffers. Width, at 6'6", was six inches more than the passenger carriages. Roofs were arched but lacked the

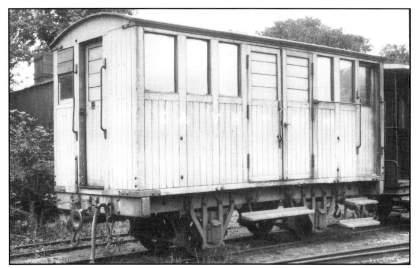

Brake van No 1, photographed on the same day as the top photograph on page 69. Comparison with the diagram on page 86 is interesting. In the photograph the two doors which open outwards are not glazed and neither is the end door of the vehicle.

LGRP 7118

bowed ends of the carriages. The maximum height was 9'6". The sides were straight and were without the tumble-in at the bottom shown by all five carriages, presumably because maximum floor area was wanted. There were eight small rectangular windows on each side, and three more at the ends. Each end had a central glazed door, sliding in the case of No 1, but in No 2 hinged to open inwards, the hinges being on the near side. A further difference between the vans was a glazed outward-opening door on the side of No 1, at the right end of the offside (ie next to Victoria Bridge). Both vans had a double outward-opening door, 4'3" in width, positioned centrally in the off-side. In the case of No 1 at least, photographs towards the end show that the outwardly opening doors were no longer glazed. Both vans were rebuilt in 1908 and No 2 again in 1929. These detail differences possibly date from these rebuildings. According to Glover's Diagram Book, No 1 was 'in good order' in January 1930, though 16 months earlier it had needed a new set of tyres, new roof supports, repainting and repairs to the brake gear, altogether estimated to cost £25. At that same time No 2 van required a general rebuild and a set of new tyres at a cost of £89. The handbrake wheels were situated in the near-side east corner of each vehicle. Westinghouse brake gear was also fitted. The four 2'3" wheels were set at 7'0" centres.

Wagons No 1 to 14 were originally goods vans, built by Oldbury in 1884. These had small ventilators at the top and flaps at the bottom, which were opened when cattle were carried and closed when dry goods were carried. However, it is possible that the dual purpose nature of these vehicles dates from their rebuilding in 1903-12 and that, prior to that, they were simply goods vans.

Nos 15 to 20 were open wagons of the same vintage. A further order, placed in 1890, as traffic developed, was for open cattle wagons Nos 21 to 23. Nos 21 and 22 were rebuilt as dual purpose covered vans in 1921 and 1917 respectively. A bogie open wagon, No 24, came in 1896. Three covered cattle wagons, Nos 25 to 27, were added in 1899. These were later rebuilt as dual-purpose vans. All the above were constructed by Oldbury. Finally, in 1912, came Nos 28 and 29, both built by R Y Pickering of Wishaw, on steel underframes, No 28 a six-ton open and No 29 a fifteen-ton bogie open. Their tare weights were four and six tons respectively.

All the Oldbury wagons had timber underframes, whereas the two Pickering wagons had steel underframes. Of the 1884 roofed Oldbury wagons (Nos 1 - 14), four had handbrakes only and were piped (Nos 7, 10, 11 and 14), and the others had Westinghouse brakes. The six open wagons had handbrakes only. Of the 1890 Oldbury vehicles (Nos 21-23) only No 22 had Westinghouse fittings, the others having handbrakes only. No 24 had only a handbrake and the five remaining wagons (Nos 25-29) had Westinghouse brakes. Thus, of the 29 wagons, sixteen were fitted with the Westinghouse, while thirteen had hand brakes and were piped. This approximately half and half ratio contrasted with that of the carriages and brake vans, of which all had Westinghouse brakes. It is noteworthy that the Cavan and Leitrim and the CVBT, were the only companies in Ireland to employ the Westinghouse brakes on their rolling stock.

Wagon No 15 was unique in that the whole of one side fell. It was used for conveying mill stones and grind stones, which were quarried in the Castlederg district [2]. Being for specialised traffic it saw less use than the others.

The livery of the goods vehicles was grey with black ironwork and white lettering: 'C&VBT Co' was in block capitals accompanied by the serial number. Tare weight was given as '3-17-0' and capacity as 'Load 6 tons'.

The first recorded wagon rebuild was done in 1901, when two

This is a poor quality, but rather interesting, view of No 12 as built in 1884. The picture would lend weight to the view that wagons Nos 1-14 were originally vans, rather than dual purpose vehicles. The ventilators seen in the later photographs are absent here, but the door design and the ribbing at waist level correspond to what we see in the picture of No 6 in 1930.

Michael Pollard collection

wagons, Nos 6 & 17, were brought into the shops. In the decade (1901 - 1910) five wagons were rebuilt. In the succeeding decade (1911-19) fourteen wagons were taken into the shops for attention. The years 1911-13 saw the rebuilding programme actively pursued under W H Holman, when eleven wagons went through the repair shop. In 1914 only No 24, the Oldbury open bogie wagon, got attention. The following two years were blank, either due to wartime shortages of material or possibly due to tradesmen being in HM Forces. By the time matters were back to normal, the 1921-30 decade saw eight wagons go through the shops. By then financial stringency brought rebuilding to an end and repairs were confined to re-tyring. The following table summarises wagon repair work from 1901 onwards:

1901 Nos 6, 17	1917 No 22
1903 No 8	1918 No 10
1904 No 16	1921 Nos 21, 24
1907 No 7	1923 No 23
1911 Nos 1, 5, 9, 13	1926 Nos 17,19
1912 Nos 2, 11, 12, 14	1928 Nos 25, 26, 27
1913 Nos 3, 4, 18	1929 No 20
1914 No 24	

The 1924 Annual Report shows, under 'Maintenance and Renewal of Rolling Stock', a charge of £769-19s-9d against 'Rail Motor Coach'. This would be for labour and materials incurred in its construction and, no doubt, accounts for the fact that no wagon repairs were done in 1924 and 1925.

No photographs have been seen showing grids on the wagons (Nos 1-29) or on the brake vans (Nos 1-2). This is confirmed in G T Glover's sketch book and it would appear that they were not fitted with skirts.

The typical order in which vehicles were marshalled in mixed trains can be seen in photographs and was as follows: Engine, flat wagons, covered wagons, carriages, brake van.

Opposite: In contrast, No 2, rebuilt in 1912, is typical of most of this type. Here the doors have been given external vertical planking rather than internal horizontal . and the waist level ribbing has gone. When carrying cattle the upper ventilators and lower drainage gaps were opened. The hand brake is on in this view but off in the upper.
LGRP 7119

Dual purpose cattle wagon and goods van No 6 in 1930. Whilst most of these vehicles were as shown below, No 6 exhibits features which clearly go back to their 1884 form. This vehicle was rebuilt in 1901 and was therefore one of the earliest to be altered.

LGRP 7120

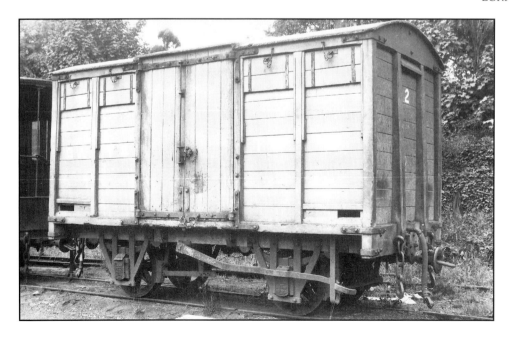

Left: Dual purpose van No 14 seen at Victoria Bridge. This view shows the end detail and the draw gear, chains and air pipe. All these wagons had timber frames.

Dr H A Whitcombe

Above: Nos 25 and 13 at Aughnacloy on 25 June 1937, after sale to the Clogher valley Railway. Note the corrugated sheeting on No 25, no doubt a repair job on a leaking roof. No 25 was one of the 1899 Oldburys and was originally a dedicated cattle wagon.

H C Casserley 14199

Six ton open wagon No 28, built by Pickering in 1912. This wagon was a one off and had a steel under frame.
Michael Pollard collection

The final vehicle in the CVBT fleet was No 29, another 1912 Pickering vehicle. It was a 15 ton bogie vehicle.
Michael Pollard collection

Appendix I

—

Notes on tickets by C R Gordon Stuart*

The earliest tickets of this company, when the line opened in 1884, were very smart and well produced card tickets. First class were white and third class green. They conformed to customary railway practice of having issuing and destination stations clearly shown and the initials of the company at the top of the ticket, after the conditions of issue, as was originally the case with many ticket issues of the LNWR in Britain. About 1900, a new system was introduced, which may have been in operation for some time, concurrently with the normal card tickets. That was to issue upright card tickets, headed with the company's full title, for different fares, although these tickets were for different classes also.

The first class were as follows:

1s 0d	Yellow with three red stripes
9d	Mauve, with one vertical red band
6d	Mauve only
3d	Mauve, with three horizontal red stripes

The third class were:

8d	Blue
6d	White
4d	White with vertical blue band
3d	White with diagonal red band
2d	Green with vertical orange band

The first class 1s 0d and the third class 8d only mentioned stations, as above the fare they stated 'From Victoria Bridge to Castlederg'. Second class was never provided. The last issue of this system before it closed were all of the 'bus type', with destinations indicated by punch mark and only third class were issued. Singles, two-day returns and special day returns alone, being used and the colours were either pink or green.

It is interesting to observe that the Castlederg and Victoria Bridge Tramway used the Sloper's dating press on its tickets, by which means the date was punched out of the ticket in a serious of small holes, which could be easily read by holding the ticket up to the light.

*This Appendix is reproduced from the late H Fayle's "Narrow Gauge Railways of Ireland", to which it formed Appendix No 1. The author is indebted to Mr C R Gordon Stuart for permission to make use of it.

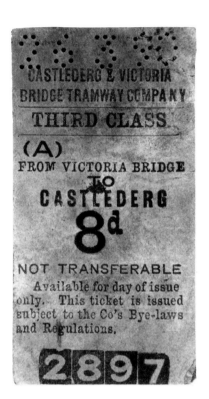

Tickets from the Castlederg and Victoria Bridge Tramway. These are not to scale. The top left ticket as an example of one using Sloper's dating press, in this case dated '26March 1890'. the two above are Edmondson card tickets, and those below are examples of 'bus type' tickets.

Plum colour

Green

Green

Appendix II

—

Note on Railway Letter Stamps*

The letter stamps initially of two pence value, were lithographed by Messrs Sealy, Bryers and Walker, and were issued in sheets of 24, arranged in four rows of six. The original design was prepared from this firm's stock design No 2 (small 'c' to conveyance), the title of the Company being then printed in and 24 (or 48) duplicated. Mr W J Davidson, Secretary and General Manager to the Company, informed me that the Company's authority from the Post Office was dated November 13th, 1897 and that 2000 stamps were probably printed.

There was only one printing but specimens are known perforated both 12½ and 10, the latter being scarce.

In stamp No 4 the lines above T of 'Tramway' are very defective. No 10 shows a white spot on the figure '2', and in No 17 there is a white spot between the shield and first 'C' of 'Conveyance'.

Additional note by E M Patterson:

Conditions as to weight and charge were changed later, the fee was increased to 3d on 15 Jan 1920 and, on 1 September 1920, the fee was raised to 4d. On 1 Jan 1928 the fee was reduced to 3d. These changes caused alterations in the stamps. In some cases new stamps of the new value were printed, in others the existing stocks were surcharged, while very often the alteration was merely made in pen and ink, or even pencil [12].

Castlederg stamps have been seen surcharged black '3' and '4' in pen and ink, while an envelope stamped with a surcharged 4d value and cancelled with a straight line *Castlederg* in purple ink, has the 1½d George V postage stamp cancelled 5 May 1925 and is in the author's possession. It is of a 'philatelic' nature.

The remaining stock of stamps, all of which were unsurcharged 2d, were removed from Castlederg. At some time they became wetted and the gummed sheets became a solid mat. Loosened by soaking, the sheets broke at the perforations, but a single sheet was rebuilt.

*Extracted from *History of Railway Letter Stamps* published by Ewen's Colonial Stamp Market, London in 1901, and compiled by J L'Estrange Ewen. This extract comprises page 334, which is illustrated by a plate showing a pair of the stamps [11].

Appendix III

—

GT Glover drawings: Engines (Scale ³⁄₁₆ " to one foot)

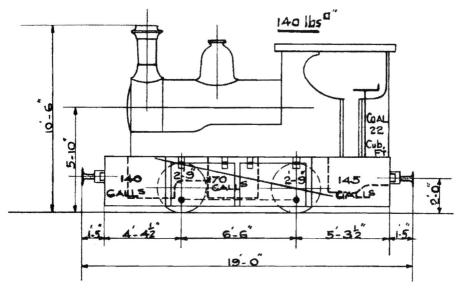

Kitson No 3. This locomotive had Walschaert valve gear. Tractive effort 7789 lbs at 85% boiler pressure.
Courtesy P Mallon

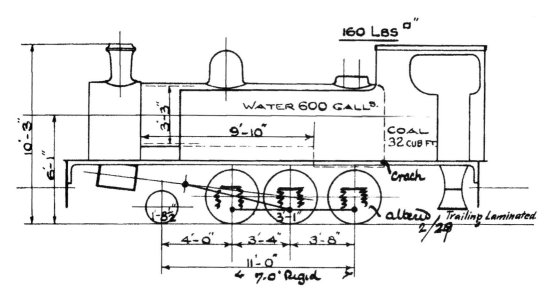

Hudswell, Clarke No 4. Allan straight link motion. Tractive effort 12,058 lbs.

Courtesy P Mallon

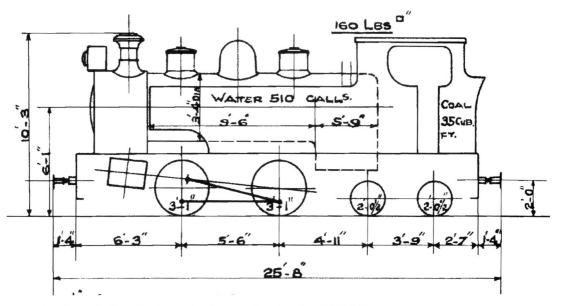

Hudswell, Clarke No 5. Stephenson's valve gear. Tractive effort 10,388 lbs.

Courtesy P Mallon

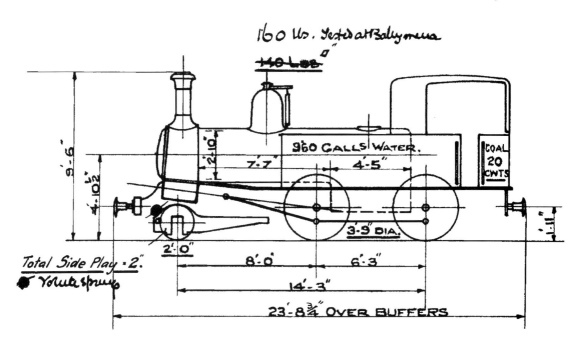

Beyer Peacock 2-4-0T. Allan straight link motion. Tractive effort 7437.5 lbs. Glover's notes say 'Engine No 3'.

Courtesy P Mallon

Appendix IV

—

GT Glover drawings: Carriages (Scale ³⁄₁₆ " to one foot)

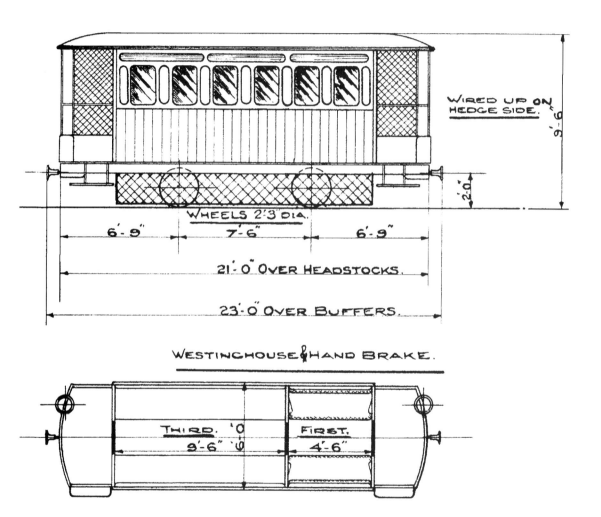

Composite carriage s 1 and 2, Oldbury 1884, seating six first class and fourteen third class.

Courtesy P Mallon

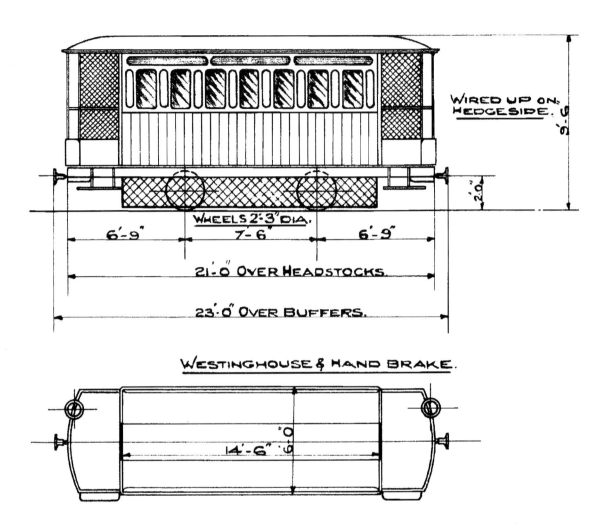

Second class carriage No 3, Oldbury 1884, seating twenty two. In 1887 it was redesignated 'third class'.
Courtesy P Mallon

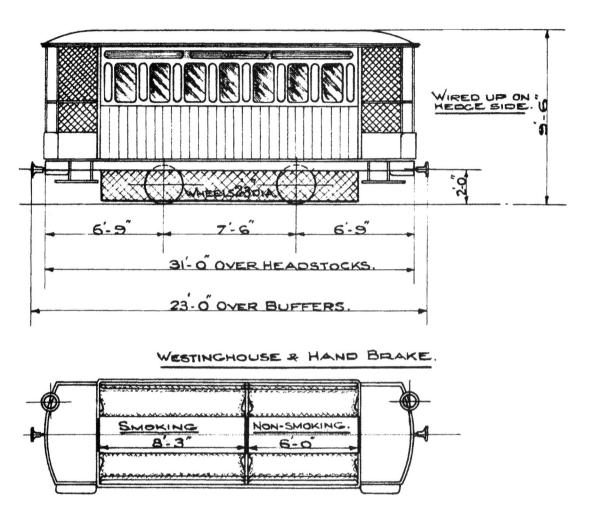

WIRED UP ON
HEDGE SIDE.

6'-9"   7'-6"   6'-9"

31'-0" OVER HEADSTOCKS.

23-0" OVER BUFFERS.

WESTINGHOUSE & HAND BRAKE.

SMOKING   NON-SMOKING.
8'-3"   6'-0"

First class carriage No 4, Oldbury 1884. The 31' 0" over headstocks length is an error for 21' 0".

Courtesy P Mallon

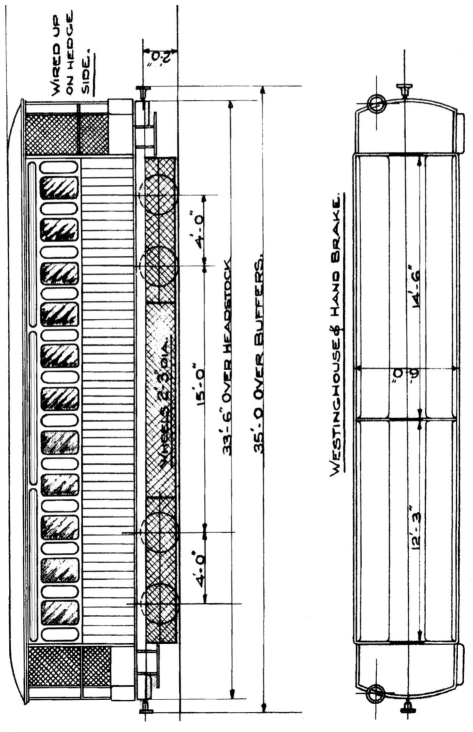

Third class bogie carriage No 5, Oldbury 1887, seating 40 passengers. Although the diagram indicates that the balconies were 'wired up' on one side, later photographs show solid sheeting.
Courtesy P Mallon

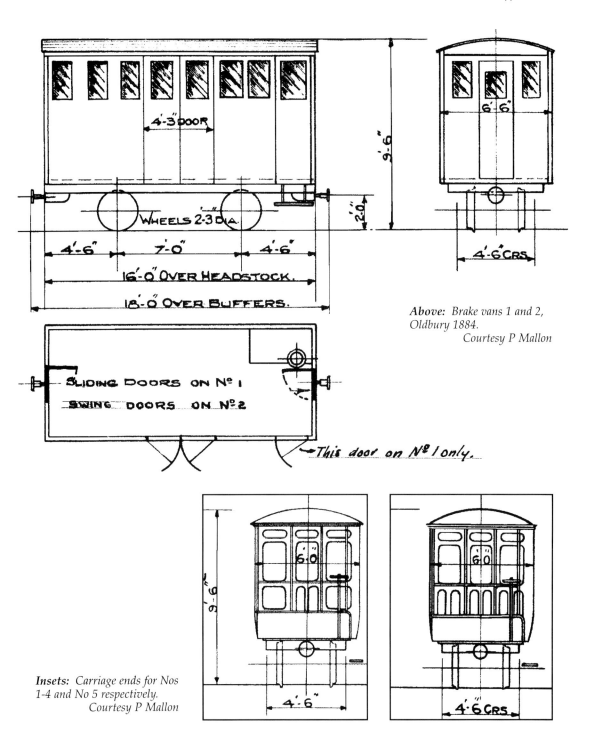

WHEELS 2-3 DIA.

4'-3" DOOR

9'-6"

2'-0"

6'-6"

4'-6" CRS

4'-6" 7'-0" 4'-6"

16'-0" OVER HEADSTOCK.

18'-0" OVER BUFFERS.

Above: Brake vans 1 and 2, Oldbury 1884.
Courtesy P Mallon

SLIDING DOORS ON No 1

SWING DOORS ON No 2

This door on No 1 only.

Insets: Carriage ends for Nos 1-4 and No 5 respectively.
Courtesy P Mallon

9'-6"

6'0"

4'-6"

6'0"

4'-6" CRS

Appendix V

—

GT Glover drawings: Wagons (Scale ³⁄₁₆ " to one foot)

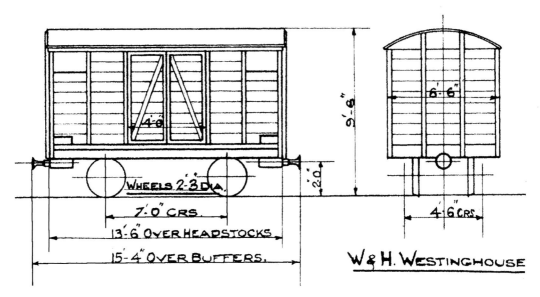

Dual purpose cattle and goods vans Nos 1-14, built 1884. Nos 21, 22, 25-27 rebuilt to this class.

Courtesy P Mallon

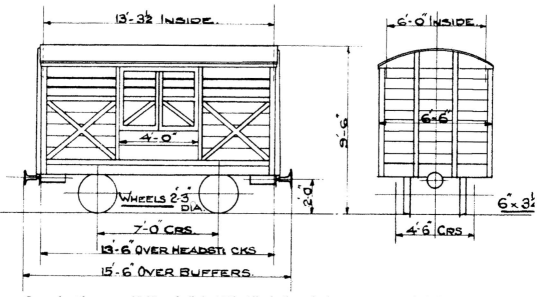

Covered cattle wagons 25-27, as built in 1899. All rebuilt as dual purpose wagons in 1928.

Courtesy P Mallon

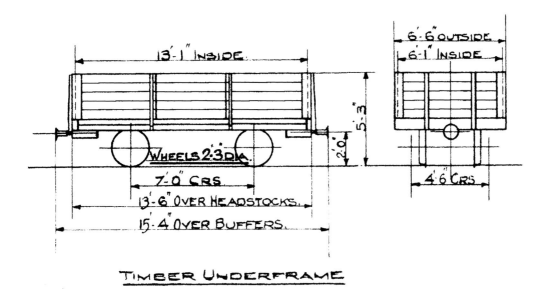

TIMBER UNDERFRAME

Open wagons Nos 15-20, Oldbury 1884. All rebuilt except No 15.

Courtesy P Mallon

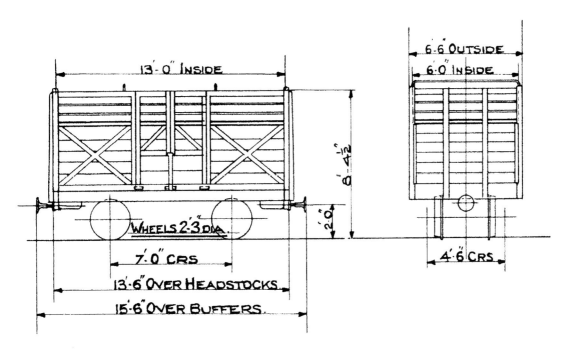

Open cattle wagons 21-23, Oldbury 1890. Nos 21 and 22 rebuilt as dual purpose covered vans in 1921 and 1917 respectively.
Courtesy P Mallon

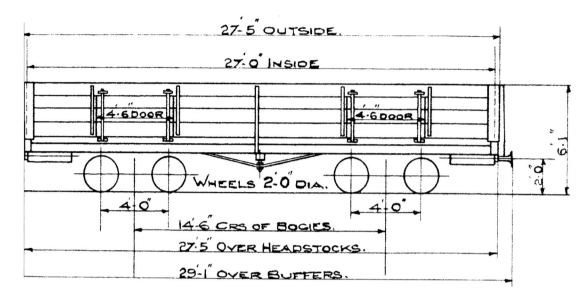

Bogie open wagon No 24, Oldbury 1896. Timber underframe, later piped. Rebuilt 1914 and 1921.

Courtesy P Mallon

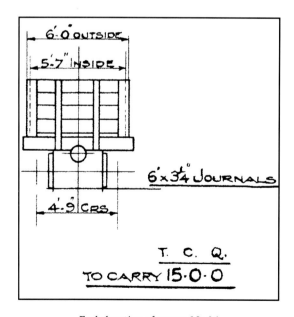

End elevation of wagon No 24

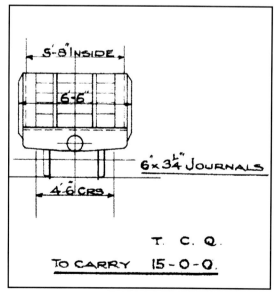

End elevation of wagon No 29

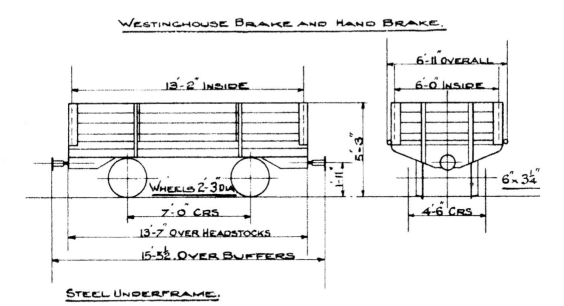

Open wagon No 28, Pickering 1912. This wagon had a steel underframe, Westinghouse brake and hand brake.   *Courtesy P Mallon*

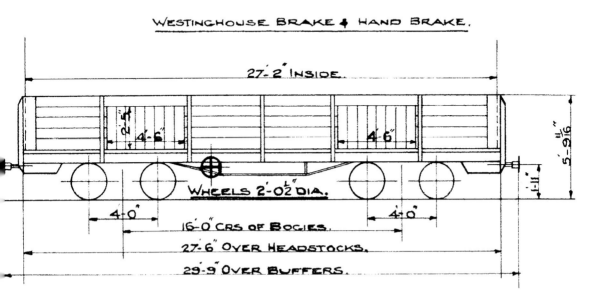

Bogie open wagon No 29, Pickering 1912. This wagon had a steel underframe, Westinghouse brake and hand brake.   *Courtesy P Mallon*

Appendix VI
—
Gradient Profile

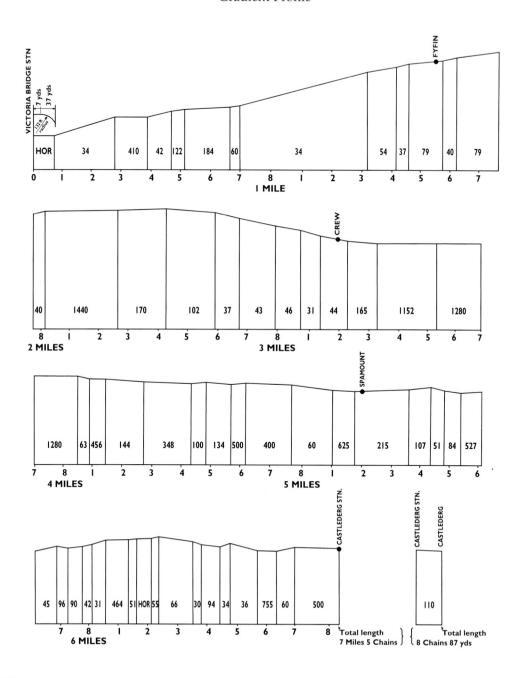

Appendix VII
—
Timetables

1899 Timetable

Down Trains.

STATIONS.	WEEK DAYS.					
	1	2	3	4	5	6
	a.m.	*a.m.	a m.	p.m.	p m.	p.m.
CASTLEDERG *dep.*	7 15	8 15	10 35	12 30	1 30	4 10
SPAMOUNT ...		8 23	10 43	...	1 38	4 18
CREW ...	Friday	8 31	10 51	C'tlederg	1 46	4 26
FYFIN ...	only.	8 38	10 58	Fairdays	1 53	4 33
VICTORIA BDGE *ar.*	7 55	8 55	11 15	only. 1 10	2 10	4 50
G.N.R. Trains.						
VICTORIA B.(G.N.)			a.m.			
for LON'DERRY,						
&c. ... *dep.*	...	9 0	11 25	...	2 14	4 57
Do. (G.N.), for						
OMAGH, &c. *dep.*	8 4	...	11 50	...	2 14	5 28
OMAGH ... *arr.*	8 28	...	12 20	...	2 44	6 1
STRABANE ,,	...	9 10	11 35	...	2 23	5 7
LONDONDERRY ,,	...	9 45	12 20	...	2 50	5 40

* On Fridays this train will not leave Castlederg till 8 42 a.m.,
and will not stop at intermediate Stations.

Up Trains.

STATIONS.	WEEK DAYS					
	1	2	3	4	5	6
G.N.R. Trains.	a.m.	a.m.	a.m.	a.m.	p.m.	p.m.
LONDONDERRY *dep.*	7 30	...	11 0	...	1 30	4 40
STRABANE ,,	7 53	...	11 35	...	2 0	5 13
OMAGH ,,	...	8 30	10 58	...	1 47	4 30
VICTORIA B.(G.N.)						
from OMAGH,&c. *a*	...	9 0	11 25	...	2 14	4 57
Do. (G.N.), from						
L'DERRY, &c. *arr.*	8 4	...	11 50	...	2 14	5 28
VICTORIA BDGE *dep*	8 5	9 5	11 50	2 15	2 25	5 35
			p.m.			
FYFIN ...		9 22	12 7	...	2 42	5 52
CREW ...	Friday	9 29	12 14	C'tlederg	2 49	5 59
	only.			Fairdays only.		
SPAMOUNT ...		9 37	12 22	...	2 57	6 7
CASTLEDERG *arr.*	8 40	9 45	12 30	2 55	3 5	6 15

Castlederg and Victoria Bridge Tramway Company.

TIME TABLE.—From 2nd JULY, 1928,

And until further Notice.

THE DIRECTORS GIVE NOTICE that the Company do not undertake that the Trains shall start or arrive at time specified in the Bills, and they will not be accountable for any loss or inconvenience which may arise from delay or detention.

THE ARRIVAL TIME—denotes when Trains may be expected, and THE DEPARTURE—that Trains will not start before time appointed.

DOWN TRAINS.—Week Days.

		a Motor Coach. A.M.	b Motor Coach. A.M.	A.M.	Motor Coach. P.M.	Motor Coach. P.M.	Motor Coach. P.M.
CASTLEDERG	dep.	7 15	8 10	10 40	1 40	3 50	6 10
SPAMOUNT	,,	—	8 16	10 48	1 46	3 56	6 17
CREW	arr.		8 23				
,,	dep.	—	8 24	10 56	1 52	4 2	6 24
FYFIN	,,	—	8 27	11 3	1 57	4 7	6 30
VICTORIA BRIDGE	arr.	7 40	8 40	11 20	2 10	4 20	6 45

a On Tuesdays and Fridays only.
b On Castlederg Fair Day this Train *will not* leave till 8.45 a.m.

UP TRAINS.—Week Days.

		c Motor Coach. A.M.	d Motor Coach. A.M.	e Motor Coach. A.M.	A.M.	Motor Coach. P.M.	Motor Coach. P.M.	Motor Coach. P.M.
VICTORIA BRIDGE	dep.	7 45	8 5	9 5	11 40	2 25	4 40	7 30
FYFIN	,,	—	8 18	9 18	11 57	2 38	4 53	7 43
CREW	arr.		8 23		P.M.			
,,	dep.	—	8 24	9 24	12 4	2 43	4 58	7 48
SPAMOUNT	,,	—	—	9 29	12 12	2 49	5 4	7 54
CASTLEDERG	arr.	8 10	8 35	9 35	12 20	2 55	5 10	8 0

c Tuesdays only.
d Fridays only.
e On Castlederg Fair Day this Train *will not* leave till 9.30 a.m.

Motor Coach—No heavy Luggage can be accepted.

On Castlederg Fair Day a Special Train will leave Castlederg at 1.15 p.m. with Live Stock, returning from Victoria Bridge at 2.50 p.m.

EXCURSIONS.

CHEAP EXCURSION TICKETS will be issued from CASTLEDERG as under :—

To LONDONDERRY and STRABANE—Excursion Tickets, available for return following day.
Fares—Londonderry, 1st Class, 7/-; 2nd Class, 5/6; 3rd Class, 4/2.
Strabane, 1st Class, 3/-; 2nd Class, 2/6; 3rd Class, 1/11.

To BELFAST—On Tuesdays, by 7.15 and 10.40 a.m. Trains, available for return on following Thursday.
Fares—1st Class, 16/9; 2nd Class, 13/9; 3rd Class, 11/4.

To ALL STATIONS—On Saturdays, available for return up to and including following Monday.
(10 Miles distance and over) Fares—Single Fare and one-third.

To ALL LOCAL STATIONS—Excursion Tickets, available for return day of issue only, at Single Journey Fare.

W. J. DAVIDSON, Secretary.

CASTLEDERG,
13th June, 1928.

Printed at the Londonderry Sentinel Office. 13628

Castlederg and Victoria Bridge Tramway Company.

TIME TABLE.—From 1st JANUARY, 1929,

And until further Notice.

THE DIRECTORS GIVE NOTICE that the Company do not undertake that the Trains shall start or arrive at time specified in the Bills, and they will not be accountable for any loss or inconvenience which may arise from delay or detention.

THE ARRIVAL TIME—denotes when Trains may be expected, and THE DEPARTURE—that Trains will not start before time appointed.

DOWN TRAINS.—Week Days.

		a A.M.	b A.M.	A.M.	P.M.	P.M.	P.M.
CASTLEDERG	dep.	7 15	8 10	11 0	1 40	3 50	6 10
SPAMOUNT	,,	—	8 18	11 8	1 48	3 58	6 18
CREW	,,	—	8 26	11 16	1 56	4 6	6 26
FYFIN	,,	—	8 33	11 23	2 3	4 13	6 33
VICTORIA BRIDGE	arr.	7 55	8 50	11 40	2 20	4 30	6 50

a On Tuesdays and Fridays only.
b On Tuesdays and Fridays this Train *will not* leave Castlederg till 8.45 a.m.

UP TRAINS.—Week Days.

		c A.M.	d A.M.	P.M.	P.M.	P.M.	P.M.
VICTORIA BRIDGE	dep.	8 5	9 5	12 5	2 25	4 40	7 30
FYFIN	,,	—	9 22	12 22	2 42	4 57	7 47
CREW	,,	—	9 29	12 29	2 49	5 4	7 54
SPAMOUNT	,,	—	9 37	12 37	2 57	5 12	8 2
CASTLEDERG	arr.	8 45	9 45	12 45	3 5	5 20	8 10

c Tuesdays and Fridays only.
d On Tuesdays and Fridays this Train *will not* leave Victoria Bridge till 9.30 a.m.

On Castlederg Fair Day a Special Train will leave Castlederg at 1.15 p.m. with Live Stock, returning from Victoria Bridge at 2.50 p.m.

EXCURSIONS

CHEAP EXCURSION TICKETS will be issued from CASTLEDERG as under :—

To LONDONDERRY and STRABANE—Excursion Tickets, available for return following day.
Fares—Londonderry, 1st Class, 7/- ; 2nd Class, 5/6 ; 3rd Class, 4/2.
Strabane, 1st Class, 3/- ; 2nd Class, 2/6 ; 3rd Class, 1/11.

To BELFAST—On Tuesdays, by 7.15 and 11.0 a.m. Trains, available for return on following Thursday.
Fares—1st Class, 16/9 ; 2nd Class, 13/9 ; 3rd Class, 11/4.

To the PRINCIPAL G.N.R. STATIONS—On Saturdays, available for return up to and including following (50 Miles distance and over) Monday. Fares—Single Fare and one-third.

To ALL LOCAL STATIONS—Excursion Tickets, available for return day of issue or following day, at Single Journey Fare.

WEEK-END TICKETS issued to Dublin, Belfast, and Londonderry on Fridays.

W. J. DAVIDSON, Secretary.

CASTLEDERG,
19th December, 1928.

Printed at the Londonderry Sentinel Office. 201928

Appendix VIII Samples of Company Stationery

TELEGRAMS: "TRAMWAY, CASTLEDERG."

Castlederg and Victoria Bridge Tramway Company.

Referring to your

Refer to in your reply

M

Secretary and General Manager's Office,

CASTLEDERG.

21st December, 19 32.

To Geo.T.Glover,Esq.,

Loco.Engineer,

Great Northern Railway Co.,

DUNDALK.

Dear Sir,

RAIL MOTOR COACH.

With reference to your letter of 17th instant.

I brought the your offer for purchase of Coach Body &c. before my Directors at their meeting on 19th instant, I was instructed to write you, that although willing to part with the Coach they think the figure offered too small. It may be of only scrap value whilst lying here, but, it will be of very greatly more value to a purchaser to make use of it.

The Roller Bearings (SKFCo.), which are in perfect order on the wheels cost more than the £25. offered.

After all I think that we are entitled to get something more out of the sale, so that this Company won't loose all and another Company gain all in the transaction. It is therefore hoped that you will use your good offices to get a better price.

Wishing you the full compliments of the season.

Yours faithfully,

W. J. Davidson

Above: Letter from W J Davidson to G T Glover, on Company notepaper, relating to the disposal of the railcar.

CASTLEDERG AND VICTORIA BRIDGE TRAMWAY COMPANY.

CONSIGNMENT NOTE. *CASTLEDERG Station, _____ 192*

The Castlederg and Victoria Bridge Tramway Company will please receive and forward, on the conditions stated on back hereof, the undermentioned Goods, consigned to

M _____

Destination, _____

via_____ per _____ Train. Time Received, _____

Sentinel, Derry—23931

No. of Articles.	DESCRIPTION.	WEIGHT.				Charges Paid on.			Who to Carried
		T.	c	q.	lbs	£	s	d	

Wagon No._____   Signature of Sender,_____

Loader,_____   [SEE BACK.

References

1 Lacy, B et al (1983) *Archeological Survey of County Donegal,* Lifford

2 Symes, R G (1891) *Memoir of the Geological Survey of Ireland:* Sheets 31 & 32 of the Maps,HMSO

3 Hutchison, W R (1951) *Tyrone Precinct,*Dundalk

4 Thomas, M D (1952) *Communication in mid-Ulster,* Ulster J Arch 15, 119-128.

5 Newham, AT (1959) *The Castlederg & Victoria Bridge Tramway,* Journ IRR Soc 5, 153-168.

6 Casserley, H C (1974) *Outline of Irish Railway History,* Newton Abbot.

7 Kidner, R W (1954) *The Light Railway Handbook,* Lingfield

8 Fayle, H (1946) *Narrow Gauge Railways of Ireland,* London & Bedford.

9 Patterson, E M (1972) *The Clogher Valley Railway,* Newtown Abbot.

10 Patterson, E M (1965) *The Ballycastle Railway,* Newtown Abbot.

11 Ewen, H L E (1901) *History of Railway Letter Stamps,* London.

12 Brummell, G (1948) *Railway Letter Stamps* in *The Encyclopedia of British Empire Postage Stamps,* Vol 1, pp 206-211, London.

13 Livesey, R M (1912) *Rolling Stock on the principal Irish Narrow Gauge Railways.*

14 McNeill, D B (1956) *Ulster Tramways and Light Railways. Transport Handbook No 7,* Belfast Museum & Art Gallery p20.

15 McDowell, J H (1931) *The Castlederg & Victoria Bridge Tramway. The loco Rly Carr & Wgn. Review,* Vol 37, 214-215.

16 *Narrow Gauge Railways in Ireland, Railway Magazine,*(1904) Vol 14, 508-514.

17 Casserley, H C *The C & VBT. The Locomotive Railway Carriage & Wagon Review,* 15th April 1931, Vol 37, 137-139.

18 *Narrow gauge locomotive for the Castlederg and Victoria Bridge Railway, The Locomotive,* 15 January 1910, p 9.

Acknowledgments

The preparation of this little book has taken considerably longer than I had at first hoped. Much of the delay stemmed from the fact that the Minute Books of the Board of Directors were neither available nor in existence. In their absence the official C&VBT general arrangement diagram book, formerly the property of the late G T Glover, Great Northern Locomotive Engineer 1912-1933, was made available on extended loan by Mr Paddy Mallon of Dundalk, and proved to be of great value.

Particular thanks are due to Richard Casserley (Berkhamstead), Mr J A A Crockett (Castlederg), Mr George Davidson (Castlederg and Bangor), Dr G F V Leary (Castlederg), Mr McGolderick (Castlederg), Mr T McDevitte (Belfast), Col Sir Basil McFarland Bt (Londonderry), Mr James J W Whyte (Londonderry), Mr Michael Pollard (Omagh) and his wife Mrs Aileen Pollard, Mr Robert Porter (Castlederg), and Mr H E Wilson (Dundalk). To that list must be added the staff of the Public Record Office in Belfast. Dr D B McNeill (Newtownards) contributed interesting and valuable information on competitive bus services.

Index